EACH CHILD A CHALLENGE
HOW TO HANG IN WHEN YOU WANT TO WALK OUT

LINDSAY R. CURTIS, M.D.

BOOKCRAFT, INC.
Salt Lake City, Utah

Library of Congress Catalog Card Number: 82-74519
ISBN O-88494-479-4

First Printing, 1983

Lithographed in the United States of America
PUBLISHERS PRESS
Salt Lake City, Utah

CONTENTS

Acknowledgments

I am most indebted to my sweetheart and wife of forty-three years for patient support and intelligent suggestions.

Dr. Wayne J. Anderson, with whom I coauthored the book *Living, Loving, and Marrying,* has generously permitted me to reprint some of his material from that book.

Mary Reeve is the kind of professional typist that every author should be privileged to have at his side to rapidly type, correct, and translate his sometimes challenging copy. To her I am indebted for the final manuscript as well as the repeated drafts of this book as it was being written and rewritten. My generous applause and thanks to her.

Introduction

No one said it would be easy to be a conscientious parent, and it isn't. Sometimes the sweet little boy or girl grows up to be an obnoxious teenager who seems to live for himself alone. Some even forsake their moral and religious training and choose (at least temporarily) the downward path. Fortunately some restore our faith in humanity's divine origins by a sane and happy approach to those otherwise awesome years of youth.

In other words, the trite expression is true—each child is different. How we handle those differences as parents has a tremendous bearing on the development of each of our offspring's character and personality. This book suggests some approaches and methods I have found or observed to be effective.

In all the range from the willing to the wayward, each child is a challenge. His years of growth tax in varying degrees the parents' physical, mental, and emotional resources. Nor will the utmost parental concern, skill, and effort always ensure the proper outcome. The child's agency is paramount and will prevail. Disappointed parents must somehow learn to live with this situation—and do so, when the going is rough, without mistakenly censuring themselves. The book offers suggestions on this important aspect of parental response, among others.

The book is written simply and in layman's language. It is my hope that somewhere within its pages all parents will be able to find help and encouragement, whatever particular needs may confront them from time to time as they face the challenge of rearing their family.

PART ONE

UNDERSTANDING THE PROBLEM

CHAPTER ONE

FROM WHOSE VIEWPOINT?

Our two-year-old grandson was climbing up to my lap. This was only a momentary whistle-stop on his busy itinerary as he made hurried rounds of everything and everybody in sight. Suddenly he paused, and I became aware of his studied scrutiny of my face.

At first I wondered if I had a smudge of dirt on my face, a piece of food on my lip, or something frightfully weird that had so intensely attracted his short span of attention. Abruptly he lowered his head in order to take a sharper look, would you believe, up my nose. Next he inspected the underside of my chin, then promptly plunged a probing finger into my ear.

Standing with his feet in my lap, he discovered that I did have *some* hair farther back on my head—hair that he quickly checked out by running his tiny fingers through its thinning strands. Sliding down my legs and onto the floor once more, he scampered away.

The thought occurred to me just what I must look like to a two-year-old. I wondered what a TV camera would have shown if it had portrayed a child's-eye view as it was aimed up my nose, or scanned the bottom of my chin, or narrowed its field to include only my bald forehead. How would my ears look from the angle of a two-year-old's probing fingers, and how would double chins look from a necktie vantage point? Or let the TV camera look through a two-year-old's eyes as he sees only the underside of tables, chairs, and drawers.

Small wonder that a child is always reaching upward and into drawers to explore the contents he can't see otherwise. The entire world most assuredly has a unique appearance for a two-year-old.

Even when that two-year-old has reached the physical stature of a teenager, he still may see the underside of many situations simply because he has not reached his full height mentally, emotionally, or spiritually. Before criticizing a youth or labeling his behavior as misconduct, let's try to understand his point of view. The "why" of his actions may be more important than the "what" of them.

While shopping once I discovered an interesting label fastened to the inner side of a particular brand of trousers. It read: "This garment is sewn and professionally laundered to give the look of being old and worn. Flaws and imperfections are part of the desired look."

According to modern peer opinion, the more worn and imperfect the garment, the more desirable it is. The trousers had been bleached to appear as though they had been repeatedly washed and faded in the sun. Purposely the bleach was spotted and uneven.

In addition to this built-in worn look, the wearer, almost as soon as he had purchased the trousers, would probably cut them off in a jagged manner to give them a "casual" appearance. To complete the "desired" look, some ragged, soiled, threadbare sneakers must also be worn. A few years ago pieces of clothing in such unthinkable condition not only would have been spurned, but quickly would have been relegated to the trash can.

In the eyes of modern youth, however, this is the desired look; and before we pass our own biased judgment upon such appearance, we had better realize that usually such a youth is merely trying to be in style. He isn't necessarily trying to be ornery, troublesome, contrary, or even disobedient. He merely wants to look like his peers.

I can remember during my own youth when my parents thought that my corduroys were terribly soiled and badly in need of washing, yet it was the style at the time to wear "cords" as soiled as possible. Nor could my parents understand why I had my curly hair cut off in favor of a flattop crew cut. Long hair at that time was "far-out" or "weird" where young people were concerned, as a crew cut would be by present standards. Do we judge our young people by our standards or theirs?

This kind of generation difference in standards can lead to problems between parent and child. Sometimes the parent will even categorize the offspring as wayward. But when we say a child is wayward, what do we mean? Wayward compared to whom? Comparisons are dangerous for many reasons. No two children are exactly alike. Each has strong points, and each has weak points.

Sometimes it depends upon where parents place the emphasis. One mother lamented the fact that one of her many children had chosen not to be active in the Church. Then with a glow of love in her voice she said: "But he is the kindest, most attentive, most compassionate child of all. He is constantly looking after our well-being." Is that son wayward? He scores pretty high in things that count. And what about the other children in the family who are so active in the Church but not as kind, considerate, or compassionate with their mother?

We speak so much in our Church about perfection. If perfection were a state of being, then there would be no further progress from that static state. Such is not the plan of God. Perfection for man is a process, an active, ongoing process. Perfection is a never-ending struggle-filled journey. Although the Lord has provided guideposts along the way, countless hardships as well as many rewards are the unmistakable lot of all travelers. Every traveler is likely to slip and slide backwards at times along the way.

But it is unlikely that anyone, even the most saintly human beings, can achieve perfection in everything—and certainly not right away. We find some commandments simple to obey, yet others so terribly difficult.

To fail in one commandment or in one particular effort does not imply that the individual is a failure. He has merely failed for the moment in one particular area of endeavor.

The Prophet Joseph Smith failed on several occasions and had to be chastened several times by the Lord. That does not mean he was a failure. He had to learn and to grow and to develop so that the

Lord could use him in the important work of the Restoration. He certainly did not become a prophet of stature all of a sudden. He was not an instant leader just because he had been blessed with a vision.

Even though we have the most noble aims and desires, we are still human and must realize that the best of us has weaknesses and the poorest of us has virtues.

Every parent would like his children to be the best in everything. In fact, many parents try to *insist* that their children excel.

Surely our Father in Heaven must have instructed Lucifer with love, ability, and power. Undoubtedly he taught him the highest ideals and most promising principles possible. No doubt our Divine Father must have tried to inspire Lucifer to be obedient, to achieve, and to excel.

The record states that Lucifer was a "son of the morning," a brilliant child of God. But even God himself would not interfere with his son's free agency, his right to choose for himself, even though his unwise choice must have broken his Father's heart.

By any standards, Lucifer was wayward. Certainly many earthly children can become so, or at least become "problem children," if they are not properly reared or if they use their agency unwisely. That's where parents come in. We are entrusted with the steward-ship of our children. As parents we certainly want to be alert to any warning signals, to any signs that our children are having problems or need special help. And there are some warning signals in rearing children, just as there are warning signals in my car.

For instance, as soon as I turn on the ignition key in my car a soft, pleasant chime sounds, warning me to buckle up my seat belt. Until I close the car door a buzzer reminds me that I can't drive safely with a door that is not completely closed.

If the key is left in the ignition when I leave the car, another buzzer informs me, "You forgot to remove your ignition key." When the fuel tank has only five or six gallons remaining, a tiny light flashes to remind me to stop at the next service station.

If the car's motor becomes overheated or if the generator is not returning sufficient power back into the battery, red warning lights tell me so. If I leave lights on in the car, a warning buzzer lets me know of my negligence. Another light even tells me when the windshield washer fluid is at a low level. A security mechanism honks the horn and flashes lights if someone tries to break into my car.

There are several ways we can view these warning "watchmen." We can allow the buzzers to bug us. We can let flashing lights fluster us. Even supersoft chimes can chew at our annoyed nerves. Many distraught drivers have had these warning devices disconnected so that they will not be reminded of their negligence. To such drivers the whole warning system is nothing but an unnecessary and annoying nuisance.

By contrast we can realize that these so-called "sorehead exasperators" actually serve only two purposes: to protect our car and possibly to save our lives. They are working only for *our* welfare.

If we neglect their heedings, the car can overheat and destroy an expensive motor. If the battery is neglected, it will fail to function just when its services are most indispensable. One evening spent in the emergency hallway of any hospital would quickly convince us of the life-saving value of buckled seat belts.

In desperation a frustrated father asked his impudent son, "Just who do you think you are?"

In all honesty the son replied, "Dad, I wish I knew."

Perhaps the most consistent trait of a typical teenager is his inconsistency. Yet this is not intentional. It is merely indicative of the internal turmoil and the emotional chaos that are taking place in his mind as he searches for his identity. To us his inconsistency may be a warning signal, a cry for help.

Sometimes he acts like a ball player trying to steal a base. He leaves second base for third; then questioning his action, he returns to second base, and occasionally is caught in between. He is trying to leave childhood behind and suddenly spring into adulthood. Not knowing what to expect, he is frightened as to his ability to handle it, yet he realizes with trepidation that there is really no turning back.

Perhaps one of the most revealing signs of this stage is a teenager whose voice has changed, who cries like the child he was only a short time ago. He is embarrassed, yet he knows he can do nothing about it. Regardless of what we say in such a situation, it will probably be wrong; the youth remains convinced that these problems plague only him and no one else on this earth. A warning signal.

In his childlike search for attention he may intentionally do everything just the opposite to what we want him to do. If all the family wants to go on an outing, he refuses to go, thus causing worry for the parents. If forced to go, he will make the trip miserable for everyone else. Clothes are acceptable only if they are unacceptable to his parents. This also may be a sign of the inner frustration at this age.

This fuzz-on-the-upper-lip stage is often plagued with acne, which in turn is plagued by an indulgent appetite for sweets and an indifferent neglect of adequate bathing. This teenager is torn between his awakening sex urges and his previous disdain for girls. To him his future is uncertain and his present is an insuperable day-to-day struggle within himself. Girls may have slightly different problems, but much of the self-doubt and many of the qualms are so similar that gender provides no immunity from suffering.

So teenagers have these problems. So what do we do about them? We suffer ourselves as we see these signs of internal agony. What can we do? The last half of this book will deal with ways to cope, to help, to understand.

Perhaps the best thing to do at this stage is to be patient. Resist the urge to do something. Listen carefully when your troubled teen-ager wants to talk. Refuse to become upset, to overreact, or to argue. What he really needs is an acoustic sounding board that absorbs everything, *including* some abuse, without throwing it all back at him.

You will recognize a little red light here, a warning chime there, indicating that he is having problems. Be aware of them, be kind, be long-suffering, be loving, be the *silent* loving type. Be available when he or she wants to talk. Listen, then talk just enough to let him know you do hear him and are interested.

This, too, will pass.

I recall a tiny, almost invisible electrically charged wire that was strung around some valuable and sacred displays to protect them from vandals. Any contact with the almost invisible wire was designed to sound a warning that visitors or viewers had ventured too close to the displays. Many people objected to these wires, not realizing that they protected both the view-pieces and viewers from what could be disastrous and costly casualties.

Each of us is born with the Light of Christ in us, a conscience whose tiny warning signals sound off to tell us when we are on shaky soil. The warning tells us we are treading on threatening territory. We can condition ourselves to ignore these warning lights, chimes, bells, and buzzers. Our ears can become deaf to them, our eyes blind to them, and our senses dulled to a point of imperception if we so desire.

One man I know has placed a strip of black tape over the seat belt light so it won't keep reminding him that he should buckle up. But deep down inside his conscience will not be silenced.

If we listen and try to understand, we will be blessed with discernment that may help us avoid many costly, uncomfortable, and even disastrous dilemmas in life. Yes, warnings are blessings sent from heaven like guardian angels who want only to protect us, our families, and our welfare.

If we are prayerful and try to remain close to our sons and daughters, we parents can detect these warning signals and take action before it is too late. Let's heed the early signals that things aren't right with a son or daughter so that we can give special attention and help where and when it is needed. Let's also remember that anyone who is alive can change.

Once again, let's use the term *wayward* cautiously. Don't let it stigmatize or label a son or daughter who is merely trying to find himself or herself. Let's not call them wayward just because they do not measure up to what *we* think they should be.

You and I have no idea what the final outcome will be in this world or in the world to come. But before we label a child as a failure, we must keep faith in him and know that he can and probably will change.

Wayward has many synonyms, but in front of all of them let's place the word *temporarily*. Nothing at this point is final. Searching, looking, exploring, may describe a situation as it is today, but cannot imply what tomorrow may bring. Perhaps it would be kinder and more understanding to say that our children merely have some problems they are working out.

The game is not over until the final score is officially recorded in the books of heaven.

CHAPTER TWO

WHY DO THEY WAVER?

Accepting that any one of our children may at some time be tempted to stray in one degree or another, we may well question why this is so. What "gets into them," so to speak?

At one time our family had a small home in the country surrounded by about an acre of thick green grass. The thought occurred to us that it would be an ideal pasture for a couple of sheep.

Before the sheep had been in the pasture twenty-four hours they had already started to poke their noses through the mesh fence surrounding it. We assumed this was merely a habit that all sheep follow to scratch their noses.

I paid little attention to what they were doing until the next morning when I discovered they were gone. The *nose* holes in the fence had been enlarged until they could wriggle their entire bodies through the fence and escape.

Why would sheep want to escape from a pasture as green and lush as the one they were in? They were not tethered. They had plenty of room in which to play and cavort. Feed was plentiful. Water was handy.

After repairing the holes in the fence, I looked for and soon found the two sheep wandering lazily along the side of the road, munching grass that was not as long, as green, as thick, and probably not as delicious as the grass in their own pasture.

Because the two sheep persisted in destroying the fence and repeatedly escaping from the pasture, I soon sold them. This problem of escaping I have discussed with many farmers and especially with sheep farmers. None has been able to give me a satisfactory reason why sheep persist in escaping to something less favorable than what they already have.

Likewise, young people often have an urgent, almost compelling desire to "escape," to leave home, to get away from parents and "control." They are not sure themselves from what they want to escape. In many instances they admit that they have not really been restricted.

In vain parents search for answers, often blaming themselves when they are not to blame. They review their relationship with their children and wonder wherein they have failed. In most cases they haven't failed at all. And the conduct of their children is often as inexplicable as the persistent escape of the sheep.

On one occasion my wife and I were traveling a narrow road down a canyon when we encountered a herd of sheep. There is only one experience more frustrating than encountering a herd of sheep coming toward you on a narrow road and that is encountering a herd of sheep traveling in the *same* direction you are.

You can honk, holler, and shout. The sheep may run a little faster, but they do not get out of the way. As we neared this particular herd, we breathed a sigh of relief as they slowly crossed to one side of the road, and it appeared that we would be able to pass them. We were wrong.

Just as the last sheep had crossed the road something caused one of the sheep up front to cross back to the other side. I'm certain that the grass was no better on one side than the other. We purposely searched for some reason that this sheep should cross the road in front of us. We found none.

But true to form *all* of the sheep now decided they must also cross the road again, blindly following the first sheep who obviously didn't know why he had crossed the road either. Undoubtedly sheep feel some kind of peer pressure that forces them to follow (however blindly) where other sheep go. Impatiently we were forced to wait until the entire herd had crossed the road again.

Perhaps there is a little sheep in all of us, because we also follow blindly what others do. We style our hair, our clothes, our cars, our language, and many other habits after those whom we recognize as style-setters. Yet how often do we question or investigate the qualifications of these so-called authorities or style-setters?

The only difference between young people and adults in this game of blind "follow the leader" lies in the style or custom we are considering. You may recall the familiar line of a famous comedian: "The devil made me do it."

But the comedian's follow-up line says, "But after that I did it on my own." That is true of ourselves. Brigham Young said that the devil didn't need to lead him into temptation. "I seem to be able to find my own way there quite easily," he said.

Although we must give Satan credit for causing some of the youth to go astray, the youth must also shoulder part of the blame. Rather than maliciousness in these young people, there seems to be a stubborn resolve to be different from society, different from the establishment. And once having elected to bow to peer pressure, our youth have a difficult time breaking away from the crowd without losing face.

Have you ever heard of lemmings? These micelike creatures gather into massive groups as they stream across the countryside. Ravenously eating their way as they go, these mini-size destroyers devastate field after field of crops, leaving horrible havoc in their wake.

Lemmings have no idea where they are going. Each blindly follows the lemming in front of him. Ultimately they reach the seashore where, like a herd of buffalo stampeding off a cliff, these furry fellows follow one another into the sea. Not one of them has the good sense to perceive disaster, or the wisdom and courage necessary to buck peer pressure enough to turn either to the left or right. They simply follow the one in front of them, topple into the water, and drown.

Pretty stupid of them, isn't it? Yet some of our young people do the same thing with drugs, never pausing to look where the drugs are taking them or questioning the integrity of the peers who have introduced them into this enslaved way of life.

A newspaper account told of two teenage girls who heard that an old motel was to be torn down. "How exciting," they thought, "to sneak into that old motel and spend a night there!"

After telling their parents that each was staying at the other's house for the night, they took sleeping bags and went to the motel. During the night, they were both raped and beaten by a transient. Their thrill turned into a life-threatening, terror-filled experience.

Yes, it was stupid. But how many stupid things did we do when we were their age, and just for the "thrill" of it?

"I understand" may be more important to your son or daughter at this point than "I love you." "You may be right" may be far more acceptable than trying to lecture, counsel or warn. Resist the overpowering temptation to "soapbox" in this situation.

So often we try to remind them that we have gone through the same problems. We haven't. We think we had a tougher time when we were young than they are having. We didn't. We think we worked harder for what we received than they have to do. We didn't.

And why do I insist that they don't have it easier than we had it in our day? Simply because conditions were different in our day and therefore not comparable with theirs. Furthermore, they are not really interested in what happened in our day.

We think *our* standards haven't changed. They have. Aren't we more tolerant of sin than we used to be? Don't we watch PG movies that would have not only been censored but never permitted when we were young? Yet we condone these movies enough to pay money to see them.

Our newspapers, magazines and books are blatant with sex and violence that we not only permit but either wittingly or unwittingly digest. Remember, kids don't write the stuff. Adults do. Our standards *have* relaxed considerably. How much more will they relax with the next generation and the next?

Have you ever sipped on soup that was searing hot and had a sore tongue for days afterward? Have you noticed how only a few seconds of this searing can spoil the remainder of the meal?

By contrast, can you remember the first bite of the first peach of the season, or the first apple, or the first bite of a prepared-to-perfection steak? Makes your mouth water doesn't it? No other bite of the entire meal tastes quite as good as that first one.

Sweet, sour, bitter, or sugary, all of these sensations become gradually less "sensational" as they are repeated. How noticeable any odor of a room is when we first encounter it! Whether the special spick-and-span smell of a new car or the stale-smoke scent of a sworn smoker's vehicle, these odors register themselves right away.

But good or bad we notice them for only a short time because our olfactory nerve endings quickly become fatigued. Gradually we are "conned" into complacency. When our senses are dulled, the annoying soon becomes unnoticeable.

Likewise our spiritual senses are at first sensitive to and shocked by sin and selfishness. And have you noticed how righteous thoughts send forth a spirit that stimulates us to righteous doing? At first such thoughts seem to sharpen the taste buds of our souls.

But in a similar manner, sinful thoughts at first "burn" these same taste buds and make most thoughts that follow unpleasant and difficult to savor. But when repeated, sin pulls down the antennae of spiritual sensitivity and shrinks the soul's receptivity.

At first sin produces sensations of shame. But if sin persists, the discomfort is dulled, the agony of our indiscretion is placated, and we rationalize our wrongdoing. Sin seems to become less serious to us.

Isn't this one of the reasons the Lord has commanded that we renew our covenants regularly by attending our sacrament meetings? We need to breathe fresh air again. We need to remove ourselves from the stale smoke-filled rooms of the world and give our spiritual taste buds an opportunity to sharpen themselves again.

As parents we need this constant spiritual reminding and renewal to maintain our standards and to preserve our spiritual equilibrium. It is difficult for us, as adults, to resist this ever-present attrition and erosion of our principles. Our children expect us to be constant and unchangeable.

Three young boys camped on the edge of an eighty-foot precipice as the result of a dare. Little did they suspect that one of them would get up during the night, become confused, and slip off the cliff to his death.

So often a harmless-appearing venture turns out to be more than harrowing. Perhaps you have heard the expression "No more backbone than a jellyfish." Let me tell you how misleading this statement can be.

The Portuguese man-of-war is probably the most underrated fish in the sea. Innocuous and inoffensive appearing, it looks more like an overturned soup bowl. But underneath that bowl lies sure death for any enemy that encounters it.

Concealed under its body are some innocent-appearing threads that suddenly shoot out like spear guns and encompass any unsuspecting prey before it has any idea what is happening. Additional barbed threads quickly pierce the victim's body and pump deadly poison into it. Instant paralysis is soon followed by death.

Size means nothing when it comes to jellyfish. Whether one inch or eight feet in diameter with twenty-foot-long tentacles, the sting is the same and nearly always fatal.

We are conditioned from infancy to fear the rattlesnake's rattle and the lion's roar because they warn us of their evil intent. But young people (and many adults) too often view drugs, liquor, and crime as innocent jellyfish, something that they can take or leave as they choose. The real danger is the *lack of fear* of danger.

Just like the Portuguese man-of-war, drugs can encompass, pierce, and poison almost before a victim knows what has happened to him. You may have to become an informed parent on the subject of drugs in order to adequately discuss and/or understand this problem with your children.

Sometimes our children accuse us of being inconsistent, and at times we are. One day I watched a skilled dog trainer help a dog owner learn consistency.

For example, the owner's dog was on the sofa, and the owner yelled at his dog, "Get off the sofa!" Scared to death, the dog leaped off the sofa, and as he did so he received a swat on his behind. To the dog's mind this was punishment for doing exactly the thing the owner had commanded him to do.

The dog barked, and the owner yelled, "Shut up!" The dog thought the owner was telling him to bark, so he barked again; and so it went until the owner was exasperated. Yet the dog was being punished for doing exactly what he thought he was told to do.

How often we give mixed-up signals to our young people! We tell them not to speed, yet they see the speedometer gradually stray over the speed limit when *we* are driving. This inconsistent action says: "Don't pay any attention to what I have told you. The speed

15

limit isn't really important. Obeying the law is merely something we give lip service to.'' Perhaps we illegally get away with whatever we can on our income tax, yet we frown on covert theft by our children. Our children learn more from our example than we think. And our ''lesson'' may cause them to follow the wayward course rather than the straight one.

The commonly used phrase ''hang loose'' really means ''stop worrying about the outcome.'' But it also reminds me of a certain unique cable-car ride.

As we looked over the prospective ride up the mountain, we had some misgivings. Particularly as we studied the nearly one-mile distance between a couple of the towers. Uneasily we watched as the long, slack cables swayed back and forth. This cable car was to take us up the back side of the mountain to the sending tower for a local television station.

Before we boarded the car for the long ride, our guide had cautiously surveyed the situation to make certain it was safe.

''When there is even a whisper of wind,'' he said, ''the car sways too wide and we lose control. In breezy weather the journey is simply too hazardous to undertake at all.''

As we started out, we were intrigued by the autumn aura and the countless deer we could see scampering away from this intrusion we were making into their empire. The oak brush and maple trees were fascinatingly full of color at this time of year. A few appeared to have been just freshly painted a fire-engine red. Any danger in such a thrilling ride was the furthest thing from our minds.

About a third of the way up the mountain our cable car began swaying with a gentle batch of breeze. Suddenly we were beginning to sense how chancy this uncertain chariot could be if the wind should *really* begin to blow. Swinging in the car at this stage of the ride was thrilling, but any additional movement would have replaced fun with fear, and anticipation with anxiety. Arriving safely at the top, we quickly disembarked and determined we would *drive* down the opposite side of the mountain in a car.

How like life this is! It's adventuresome, it's intriguing, it's enticing, and certainly it's interesting to swing a little in life. And I'm not so sure the Lord doesn't want us to experience some of these ventures, as long as we keep things under control, as long as we don't break any of the rules. It certainly guarantees against boredom.

But how easy it is to become so engrossed in the thrill of the ride that we fail to notice the danger signals in the dare we have undertaken! The swinging so easily can become reckless and unrestrained. Soon control capitulates to capriciousness.

A sign along the road in the Bahamas reads: Stay Away from the Verge. In our country it would read: Beware of Soft Shoulders. There *is* danger in venturing too close to the verge. Before we know it, our tires have sunk into the soft sand at the edge of the road and we are in trouble too tight to get out of.

In any journey, we must decide if the suscitation of swinging is really worth the insecurity and the sacrifice that it ultimately might demand.

You may feel it's a justified risk if *you* are making the journey. But how do you tell a teenager or even a young adult in your family that the journey they are about to make is too hazardous for their health? How do you tell them that their "hanging loose" may really leave them just "hanging."

Probably the worst approach is to forbid them to make the journey at all. They not only have their free agency, but also they will find a way to make the trip without our permission if they are determined to do so.

If the channel of communication is open, you may be able to talk it over with your teenager. You might try properly inquiring about the venture. Don't hold an inquisition or a third-degree question-and-answer session.

"Tell me about your plans, son; I'm really interested." Or, "That sounds exciting. Tell me about it!" "You've undoubtedly thought a lot about this. How do *you* feel about the risks?" might be wisely interjected at the proper time.

Instead of dishing up advice, hold out your plate for a helping of *their* feelings on the subject. Listen to their appraisal of the situation and see if they have already considered some of the dangers. In some instances you will simply have to watch as your children make mistakes, serious mistakes, mistakes about which you can do nothing.

While you must be careful not to attach an unfair or unwarranted label on anyone, you must also have the wisdom to recognize a poisonous snake when you see one and have the courage to call it by its proper name, especially when someone's life is at stake.

Although we want to listen, to understand, and to communicate, we still must *deal* with drugs, liquor, and crime early and with all the skill possible, should our child get involved in any of these. To turn or bury our heads, to ignore, to hope that problems will go away if left to themselves, is to invite disaster and destruction among those who tamper with them.

We can attack these vices without attacking our children. We can love our children and still hate what these three are doing to them. But we must be certain, when we discuss these problems with our children, that our comments are directed at the drug, the liquor, or the crime, not at our son or our daughter.

Why do they waver? We often don't know why. And perhaps we don't have to know or understand all of the whys. But until we know, we can try to *understand* them and *love* them, because that's the only way we can help them get started on the road back.

WHOSE FAULT?

As well as asking why, when parents observe that a child is straying from the fold or is exhibiting those tendencies, the natural thing is for them to apportion blame.

Most arguments that try to determine whose fault it is are lost before they even begin. Certainly parents lose poise as well as prestige when they probe too deeply into "who" instead of "what."

The most docile cat will arch its back and cause its fur to stand on end if it is backed into a corner. A hallowed, pleasant household is often dependent upon about a dozen words a day—words that are left unsaid.

Parents have made one of the most important steps in their marriage when they learn the great no-win lesson. There does not have to be a winner and a loser every time there is a difference of opinion. And this applies to their children as well as to themselves.

Attack the problem not the person. Following is an example. Correct handling of such a situation can prevent larger problems later.

Jim asked his mother if he could miss school one day to go skiing. Neither of Jim's parents were skiers and had no love for the sport nor for the fact that Jim had taken up such an expensive sport. On many occasions they had voiced their uncomplimentary opinion of anyone who would go out in such cold weather for *any* sport.

Jim's mother could have said: "How stupid can you be? Imagine missing school to go skiing. Of course you can't. You're silly to ask." But having learned some costly lessons in communications with her children, Jim's mother wisely said: "Tell me what you have in mind."

"I have all of my schoolwork up to date," Jim said, "and even a few days ahead. I have saved enough for a lift ticket, and Bob will take his car. And besides, instead of sluffing school I came to ask your permission."

"Jim," his mother said, "I do appreciate your coming to me for permission, and I know how you love to ski. I would rather you go on Saturdays and holidays than on school days. But let me talk it over with your dad, and we'll let you know within the hour."

They did give Jim permission to go skiing for one day. Jim was rewarded for being honest with them, but he also understood that they would rather he went on Saturdays and holidays. And they limited their comments to the issue at hand. They resisted the urge to lecture or to attack him by their remarks.

Instead of setting up a contest of wills or a situation of argument, Jim's mother took time to ask what he had in mind. She gave him credit for having thought out the problem. They were able to deal with the real issues, which were lessons, finances, and transportation.

Suppose Jim had already gone skiing without permission, how might the situation be handled? "Jim, the school called yesterday and said you were absent. Tell me about it." Then listen.

After listening attentively and without accusation, ask, "What do you feel you should do about it?" Then listen some more. You'll probably be surprised at how fair Jim will be in dispensing justice and assuming responsibility for what he has done.

I recall as a boy, my mother would always send us boys (eight of us) out to the willow patch to cut our own willow with which we were to be punished. It was left up to us to decide how long and how thick the willow should be. It was our responsibility to dispense our own justice and punishment. And don't think we didn't suffer from guilt all the way out to the patch and all the way back. We knew we had done wrong and had punishment coming. (The punishment usually was not as severe as we thought it was going to be.)

When I was a lad I returned from sacrament meeting one evening and informed my mother that I was never going back to church because the meeting was too long, too dry, too much of a waste of my time. "I get nothing out of it," I complained.

She listened attentively without interruption. Then, looking me straight in the eye and without any accusation, she simply said: "I go to church to *give,* and that is why I always receive something in return." She didn't even suggest I do the same, nor did she tell me I *had* to go to church. She waited to see if I had any comment, which I didn't, and that was that. I went voluntarily and obediently to church the next week—to give, and I received.

I recall something that happened to me once. Scurrying too rapidly for good judgment, I inadvertently bumped my face and head in the doorway, bending my eyeglasses in the process and giving myself a sizable knot on the side of my head. Upset at my own clumsiness, I hurriedly straightened my spectacles enough to get by (I thought) and went on my way.

It was not long thereafter that I noticed things appeared different to me. Somehow objects were out of perspective and sometimes even out of reach. Memory of the bump on my head had long since faded when I finally realized that my eyeglasses were still crooked and my severe astigmatism was being corrected in the wrong direction. Some minor but cautious adjustments soon remedied the entire situation, and I was once more seeing things as they really are.

It became apparent to me how greatly distorted our vision of life can become by having only a slight bump on the head and a small bend in our eyeglasses.

How often in life do we receive such a bump (lump) on the head from whatever source and permit crooked eyeglasses to bend our feelings out of shape and distort our thinking and our view of life in general? Such a minor malalignment can change our entire attitude and point us in the wrong direction with catastrophic end results.

Sometimes the entire experience distorts our sense of values and perception to the point that we don't even recognize that we *are* pointed in the wrong direction. We may even begin to think that *everyone else* has a distorted view of life.

Have you ever talked to someone who had his feelings hurt many years ago—perhaps even as a child—and as a result has never been back to church? How tragic for them to let one bump on the head and bent eyeglasses distort their view (and attitude) for the rest of their lives! How sorrowful to see an entire family, even for generations, deprived of the blessings of the gospel of Jesus Christ and perhaps even eternal happiness because of such an otherwise insignificant episode!

Just as with eyeglasses, a brief, cautious, even tender adjustment can so quickly make things right again. It can make us introspective once more so that our sense of values and priorities fall into proper focus.

Also from this experience I discovered that the eyeglass frames could be straightened more easily if they were warmed up first. People with injured feelings and distorted views can often be helped more understandingly if we warm them up first with sincere concern and love.

Take a peek at yourself in the mirror to see if your eyeglasses are on straight. Warm up to the gospel of Jesus Christ, and let it help you straighten out *your* perspective and priorities.

Don't let a little crick in something as simple as your point of view prevent you from partaking of all the Lord offers you in this life and the life to come.

But what if the bump has come to your son's head? What if some unfortunate event has bent your daughter's glasses so that her view of the Church—and maybe the people in it—is distorted and unpleasant?

First of all, withhold your opinion. It hasn't been requested anyway. Listen attentively and try to sense the feelings that your son and/or daughter has. Reflect on their feelings as you put yourself in their shoes.

"I can understand how you feel. It is upsetting to have something like that happen. Tell me about it."

Most young people are fair. They are also intelligent. In many instances they make better appraisals of situations than we do. Give them a chance to be heard without your judgment or even your opinion—just your understanding.

Usually they will realize (as they discuss the situation) that their point of view could be distorted, that *their* glasses may be bent out of perspective. They are smart enough to know that one bump on the head does not make the Church untrue or impugn the entire priesthood body.

Many times all children are really seeking is a listening ear so that they can vent their feelings without condemnation, accusation, or judgment.

Most people already know they are doing wrong. They may even be punishing themselves severely for what they have done.

How do they know they have done wrong? Have you ever heard of a *spiritual* electrocardiogram?

Most people know what an electrocardiograph is, although they may not understand how it works. Actually it is a very simple machine that measures the electrical charge carried throughout the body as a result of the beat of the heart. The beat (or contraction of the heart) results from an electrical impulse sent to the heart muscle.

This charge is recorded through several different electrodes so placed on the body that they register the electrical impulse from different areas of the heart. These electrodes fail to conduct the electrical charge across areas of the heart suffering injury due to blocked blood vessels in the heart (called a coronary occlusion or heart attack) as well as in many other heart disorders. Enlargement due to heart failure and irregularity of the beat are also reported rather accurately by the electrocardiograph. The printout made by this device is called an electrocardiogram.

Doctors have come to rely heavily upon these electrocardiograms to tell them what is going on in the heart not just at the present time but also to indicate any damage that has occurred in the past. The electrocardiogram can often predict what will take place in the future, and in certain cases this information permits us to take the necessary precautions to avoid trouble.

Unfortunately some first heart attacks are fatal, and the electrocardiogram has no opportunity to warn the doctor or patient that there are impending problems in the patient's heart.

In recent years an interesting device has been designed that can be worn twenty-four hours a day by those patients who are experiencing difficulty with their hearts. This device may be compared to a continuous, ongoing electrocardiogram similar to a continuous movie. While wearing the device, an individual can be warned by an alarm that he should take nitroglycerin tablets, hurry to the hospital, summon his physician immediately, or take other prescribed precautions to save his life.

Spiritually speaking, we have a similar device that warns us when our heart is not functioning spiritually the way it should. When we are not compassionate and understanding, it makes us uncomfortable. It provides us with a spiritual electrocardiogram that tells us we need to take some spiritual nitroglycerin that will open up the spiritual blood vessels of our heart so that we think of others instead of ourselves.

When we think thoughts that are unclean, see movies that are unsavory, when we contaminate our souls with things that are unbecoming a child of God, then the spiritual electrocardiogram registers an upset, it records an irregular beat, it shows beginning spiritual heart failure. It may even indicate that we are threatened with a spiritual heart attack that could cause spiritual death.

The device that powers our continuous spiritual electrocardiogram is called the Light of Christ (our conscience), that still small voice that blesses every life (see D&C 93:2). Unfortunately some of us develop spiritual deafness and spiritual blindness, spiritual numbness and spiritual insensitivity that keep us from hearing, seeing, or feeling the irregular beat and reading the abnormal printout of the spiritual electrocardiograph.

Our teenagers usually know when their lives are not in order. They know who is at fault. Through repeated sin their spiritual senses can become dull and unreceptive to the Light of Christ within them, but we must never give up hope that the still small voice may lead them back to the right track. The last thing they need or will accept from us is preaching about the sins of which they are already aware. Leave judgment and punishment to the Lord.

For young people, one of the greatest needs in the world today is for models, good models. They need heroes of the right type; and where could they better look than to their parents?

Perhaps dad isn't the athletic type. Mom probably isn't a movie star or a beauty model. But parents do have the inside track. Whatever parents lack in physical qualities, children usually supply in esteem, love, and imagination. Unless we betray their deserved (or

24

undeserved) and exaggerated confidence, children take whatever we have and multiply it by ten just because we are their parents.

We have the obligation to be good models for them, to be their champions.

Any grade-schooler knows what show and tell means. Such an exercise is usually viewed by pupils as an opportunity to show something of interest, especially something new, unusual, or curious, to their classmates and tell all they know about it.

Undoubtedly teachers are amazed at times to discover what, in the minds of their young pupils, is "showable" and "tellable." Likewise, parents might be dismayed and betimes embarrassed at some of the unmentionable events that are recounted during this period of pupil performance.

One teacher I know executed a friendly truce with the parents of her students; the teacher agreed not to reveal what the students reported in show and tell if the parents agreed not to believe all that the children attributed to the teacher after returning home.

But show and tell may have another meaning for us as parents. So often parents complain that their counsel to their children goes unheard and unheeded because of indifference and disinterest. One parent whose son had turned his back on all parental counsel hopelessly admitted, "Everything has already been said several times."

It is true. There comes a time when everything *has* already been said. But everything has not been done unless we have reviewed our own conduct to see that we have provided the kind of example, the type of model, after which the son or daughter might pattern his or her life.

Too often we have tried telling children without showing them the way. Show and tell usually goes over better with children of any age if there is more show and less tell. As previously mentioned, never has there been a greater need for wholesome examples, for unblemished models, than now.

Let's take the effort that might otherwise be expended in determining blame or fault and use it to set a good example. Children will soon get the message as they compare their own behavior with that of their model.

One father and mother felt they had shown the proper way, but found deaf ears when they tried to tell their son anything. Their parting statement to the wayward boy was: "There are two things we cannot change. The first is that you are our son. We want you to know that we would not have it otherwise, although you may feel differently. The second is that we love you. We may not approve of what you do, but neither you nor we can change the fact that we love you deeply and with all our hearts."

When the son later "found" himself, he declared to his parents: "I guess the reason I love you so much is that you loved me when I didn't deserve it." The *show* of love and affection often succeeds where the *tell* has failed.

Now, let's talk about discipline and punishment. Certainly there is need for both at times. A child who knows no discipline in his home will have a difficult time with authority outside the home. And every child needs to learn that punishment is inevitable when any law is broken. There is no better place to learn this than at home.

But keep in mind that children know they have done wrong. If you have taught them good basic principles, they are already chastising themselves, even if not openly. Behind their facade of rebellion and supposed indifference, they may be suffering more than we suspect.

Let me tell you about an interesting machine I noticed in an office. I had studied it for a long time, wondering what function such a simple-looking machine could possibly perform. In fact, it was so simple in appearance that I was ashamed to ask what the machine was used for.

Now I marvel at the genius that conceived such an invaluable timesaver. I have yet to discover its official name. But let me tell you what it does.

Have you ever misspent time attempting to straighten a stack of disarrayed papers? Have you also bent some of the edges of the papers as you tried to rearrange them? For want of a better name, let's call this particular machine a paper straightener. That's right! All it does is take a stack of disarranged papers and straighten them up—and in a matter of just a few moments.

How does it work? It literally reshuffles a stack of helter-skelter papers as they come off the printing machine. It shakes them up;

and by so doing, it permits them to arrange themselves in perfect alignment.

You're probably ahead of me on this analogy. But isn't that what the Lord has to do to us every once in awhile—shake us up a bit in order to straighten us out, to remind us to get back into line?

Already by the fourth page of the Book of Mormon, Lehi's two eldest sons had begun to rebel against their father and also against God.

> And thus Laman and Lemuel, being the eldest, did murmur against their father. And they did murmur *because they knew not the dealings of that God who had created them.*
>
> And it came to pass that my father did speak unto them in the valley of Lemuel, with power, being filled with the Spirit, until their frames did shake before him. (1 Nephi 2:12, 14; italics added.)

Needless to say, the shaking caused them to shape up and straighten out their thinking.

Yes, sometimes the Lord has to shake us up in order to get us back into line. Verse 14 continues: "And he did confound them, that they durst not utter against him; wherefore, they did as he commanded them."

On another occasion Laman and Lemuel were about to throw Nephi into the depths of the sea, but Nephi commanded them: "... touch me not, for I am filled with the power of God, even unto the consuming of my flesh; and whoso shall lay his hands upon me shall wither as a dried weed." (1 Nephi 17:48.)

His brothers were afraid to touch him. When they had repented sufficiently, Nephi stretched forth his hand toward them, and they didn't wither, but "the Lord did shake them, even according to the word which he had spoken." (1 Nephi 17:54.)

These two rebellious brothers were often shaken up by the Lord, but never did their thinking seem to straighten out for long. Once again the Lord would have to shake them up to straighten them out.

All of us at times have been shaken up by the Lord to bring us to our senses, to straighten us up for our own good. But there is more to be learned about this shaking-up-and-straightening-out process.

Let the Lord do the shaking up and the straightening out whenever possible, especially when it comes to our children. Yes, we can pray about the problem and pray for them. We can ask the Lord to love them enough to chasten them. But from us are required a loving arm around their shoulder, a look of compassion in our eye, and an understanding in our heart.

Leave the chastening to the Lord. Our children may already be experiencing shaking up and straightening out without our knowing it.

And if there is someone to blame, let the Lord point *his* accusing finger. Of us he requires forgiveness for all.

There is another aspect that should be discussed under this chapter on who is at fault. Too many parents feel guilty when the guilt is not theirs. In many situations blame and fault are difficult to establish and really not important. If we have done our best, we should feel no guilt. But we are allowed and undoubtedly will feel anguish over a wayward child.

One of the most descriptive sentences in the entire Bible portrays the Savior's feelings as he prayed on the Mount of Olives. Followed to the Mount by his devoted disciples, he withdrew a stone's cast from them as he knelt to pray.

Visualizing the various events about to take place and reviewing these with his Father, the scripture says: "And being in an agony he prayed more earnestly: and his sweat was as it were great drops of blood falling down to the ground." (Luke 22:44.)

I have wondered what kind of *anguish* the Savior's Father must have been going through at this moment to have to *permit* his Beloved Son to endure such agony. Contemplating the cruel crucifixion to come, the Savior's loving Heavenly Father and Mother must have suffered as they anticipated such torture of a righteous and obedient son.

Surely we display great love when we sacrifice so that our children might enjoy a mission, an education, and in some cases, even the luxuries of life. The greatest test of our love, however, may be the anguish we must endure as we permit our children to endure certain painful experiences so that they may learn principles they could learn in no other way. In many instances as we anticipate the dangers in their lives we wish we could suffer in their places.

The Savior understood the plan of salvation thoroughly, since he volunteered to become its central figure; yet in Gethsemane he said: "Father, if thou be willing, remove this cup from me." He must have had some question in his mind, even if only for a fleeting moment, because he quickly added, "nevertheless, not my will, but thine, be done." (Luke 22:42.)

Just at this instant, though, how the Savior's Father must have wanted to intervene and say: "Son, you have shown your willingness to comply, to sacrifice your life, to obey. That's enough! Your unselfishness, your compassion for your earthly brothers and sisters is already evidenced by your attitude. You don't need to drink from this cup. I will remove it from you." But *he loved his son enough to permit him to suffer* because it was part of the greater plan. For some important reason that we don't understand, it must have been more beneficial for Christ to die on the cross than to live; and the Father had to suffer the anguish of seeing his son suffer.

Consider also the council in heaven. Lucifer was a son of the morning. He was a brilliant spirit with tremendous talents and a fabulous future. We don't know why, with the perfect parents and the most wholesome home environment he must have enjoyed, he chose to go against his Father's plan of salvation.

God the Father must have realized in the eternal plan of things that this was to be. Nonetheless, how this Father must have suffered! What anguish he must have felt to see this promising son of his make such a fatal mistake in judgment! What anguish he must have felt as he saw a third part of his children follow after Lucifer and his wicked decision as they turned their backs on the counsel he had given them!

When we were given the blessing of having children here upon this earth, we probably looked forward to the joys, triumphs, and successes that would come with them. But we also agreed to accept whatever sorrows, failures, and anguish that might go with them. To some parents is given an abundance of the blessings of children. To certain other parents is given what seems to be an unfair share of trouble and anguish.

A most righteous, deserving, God-fearing couple I know watched in anguish as some of their sons chose not to go on missions and some of their daughters chose not to marry worthy Church members. A more wholesome home environment, a better example of love for the Lord, could not be found than in that home.

Down the street from this couple lives an alcoholic who criticized the Church and its programs. He did all in his power to put down everything the Church stood for. He tried to dissuade his sons from going on missions, and he disapproved of temple marriage. Yet his sons went on missions, financially supported by the Church; and all his children married in the temple and have remained active.

The deserving couple expressed a sense of failure and guilt because some of their children turned their backs on the gospel that had been so much a part of their lives. Their anguish could be measured by numerous sleepless nights and harrowing hours of worrisome waiting. Their frustration is understandable, as is the anguish they share with God the Father, with Adam, with Lehi, and with many other righteous parents. A sense of failure, however, is not in order for these parents who have tried so hard and have given so much. A sense of guilt for such valiant effort is neither warranted nor proper.

No one would question the ability of Adam as one endowed not only with the wisdom but also the love, the concern, and the understanding of an ideal parent. Surely he must have wondered what had gone wrong that Cain had chosen to follow Lucifer. But any feelings of guilt or failure must be attributed to Cain and to his exercise of free agency. Cain made the choice, not Adam.

The Church programs, the activity in these programs, and family home evenings help to point the way for our children. Our example, our prayers, and our wholehearted support of our local and general authorities create an environment that will show our children the proper paths to follow.

We *are* responsible for setting a good example, but we are not responsible if our children do not choose to follow it. We *do* have a responsibility to create a spiritual environment in our homes with healthy attitudes toward the Church and its principles. We *are* responsible to teach those principles in a loving, understanding, Christlike manner. The Lord will not hold us responsible if our children choose not to follow our example or if they choose to turn their backs upon that which is right.

There is no guarantee from God that our children will do what is best for them. There is no assurance that they will follow our advice or the counsel of the leaders of our Church. They have their free agency.

Let us always stop short of any force, short of any interference with the free agency that the Lord has given our children. Depriving them of this freedom of choice is Satan's way. It accomplishes nothing except to alienate our children from us and from the Church.

Anguish is part of life. It is part of love. It is part of learning the Lord's way for his children whom he also loves and for whom he also feels, at times, great anguish.

Finally, let's leave it up to the Lord to determine any "fault." Let's keep our hearts full of love, understanding, compassion, and hope if our children choose a path other than that which we have taught them. The omniscient Father in Heaven knows *our* hearts and our efforts. He will judge wisely and fairly.

PART TWO

HANDLING THE PROBLEM

CHAPTER FOUR

PRESERVE THE SELF-IMAGE

Fortunately, not all the parent-child situations relate to "difficult" children. Pleasant, amenable young people too have situations requiring decisions, and often they want to discuss them with their parents. The nature and mode of the parental response is then immensely important.

For example, so often we think we can help our son or daughter solve a problem by minimizing it. "It's really no big deal, you know!" It really *is* a big deal to them—perhaps the biggest deal in their lives—at least for the moment.

Such a remark either presumes that we could solve the problem easily ourselves (which makes our child look stupid for not being able to solve it) or indicates that we don't really understand what is going on. Such behavior on our part immediately lowers the child's opinion of himself and frequently cuts off all communication because our son or daughter realizes that we don't sense what is going on.

Try this approach. Son: "Dad, I can't decide whether to go on to school or to get a job. I wonder about earning some money and picking up school again next year."

You are tempted to say: "No problem there. Go to school." But you suppress the urge. It *is* a problem, a big problem to him. So you listen and support by acknowledging his concern.

Father: "This is an important decision to make, isn't it?"

Son: "Yes. I've worried a lot about it and can't really decide what to do."

Father: "There are a lot of factors to consider. I can understand why this would be a problem to you."

As a parent we haven't hopped in there with a cinchy solution. You haven't preempted his right to worry over his own problem. He hasn't asked you for a decision in the matter, and you have resisted giving him an unsolicited opinion.

You have left the channels of communication open because you are genuinely concerned. Your son knows that you have *listened* because you have repeated the problem back to him. You *really do understand* why this is a problem to him.

Listen with your full attention.

Here is a comparison for you to consider. The next time you buy a new metal garbage can, place your head inside, then tap (gently) on the outside with a metal object. The reverberation will astound you as it booms louder than the high school band. More than a few seconds of such banging is nerve shattering.

Next visit a music store. Seclude yourself in one of their acoustic-lined, soundproof studios and enjoy the heavenly silence about you as you concentrate on one of your favorite tapes of music. Serene, isn't it? It almost gives you goosebumps as you recall the experience.

Isn't this truly like real life? Compare a voice-raising (almost yelling) encounter in which neither bellowing communicant listens to the other with a heart-to-heart, soft-spoken, listening, under-standing visit with the same person. I think you see what I mean.

Sue comes to her mom and says: "I wish I could decide whom I like better, Tom or Joe. Both want to get serious, and I am beginning to feel it is time to make a decision."

She hasn't asked for her mother's opinion, she has merely expressed a problem that is troubling her. Mom sees a great oppor-tunity to chirp and cheer for the fellow she likes best.

"That's an easy choice to make," she could say as she tries to pile up points in his favor (and at the same time score a put-down against her daughter).

The truth is that this is *not* an easy decision for Sue to make. And it's an important decision that could affect her entire life.

Mom is too intelligent to minimize this problem. She says: "I can see why this is a problem. Each of these young men has good things going for him.'' She drops it there.

Mother may wonder if she should have taken the opportunity to give Sue a mother's more mature judgment. She may be tempted to say: ''Tom is unmotivated. He will never amount to anything. No question about it. If I were you . . .'' But mom isn't Sue, so she bites her tongue, opens her ears, and listens with full attention as Sue verbalizes her concerns.

''Tom is better looking than Joe,'' Sue says. ''He is rather lackadaisical right now. Perhaps he isn't as mature as Joe, not as steady. But life with Tom would be more interesting. And he may achieve far more in the end.''

Mom continues to listen without comment because Sue hasn't really asked for a comment or an opinion.

''Joe is the slow, steady, always-dependable type. But I wonder if I might die of boredom due to his dullness.''

Mom tilts her head and spreads her hands understandingly—but keeps her peace.

Sue: ''I have so much more fun with Tom, but I worry about his consistency. He could make a good living, but he would be more likely to lose the money too. Joe might be a plodder, but he's a steady plodder. Sometimes a slower, steadier horse wins the race because he completes it.''

Mom: ''That's good thinking.'' (She talks about the subject, not the person.)

Sue: ''Thanks, mom, for being so understanding.''

The conversation will be resumed when Sue is ready and desires to resume it. Mom will not probe or question as to Sue's decision. She has left the channels open and knows that Sue will return when she again wants to sound out her thoughts to listening ears.

After all, Sue is the one who will have to live with Tom or Joe if she marries one of them. If mom happens to put her money on the loser, she might be posting a Not Welcome sign on the door at the home of her future son-in-law—the man she didn't choose.

Perhaps you are certain that the front-running intended spouse is a loser. The decision is still not yours to make, and your interference in the matter will probably make your son or daughter more determined to go against your unsolicited judgment. And if the marriage fails, you may be faulted because you "tried to interfere from the beginning."

Steve approaches his dad about college, wondering if he should sell his car and use the money for tuition. Dad misses the point but not the opportunity to review for the umpteenth time how tough it was when he went to school. "When I went to college, I walked. And I worked a job to put myself through school," and so on.

Steve sighs and says to himself: *Here we go again with lecture number twenty-four. Doesn't dad realize he's told me this many times before? All I did was tell him I was wondering about something, and he pushes his "lecture" button.*

Dad doesn't realize that he is merely trying to build himself up in the eyes of his son (which he is failing miserably to do), and more importantly, he is missing a marvelous opportunity to communicate with (listen to) his son. This is one of those rare, precious communications initiated by his son instead of one of the awkward attempts introduced by dad. It could have piled up some super points *for* dad instead of turning off the entire conversation.

Let's start over with the same situation.

Son: "Dad, I'll be starting college in a couple of months. I wonder if I should sell my car and use the money for tuition."

Dad: "Tell me what you had in mind."

Son: "Although I'll need transportation, I also need the money for books, clothes, and tuition. I'm just debating whether I could get by without my car."

Dad: "That is a tough decision, son." No further comment, no commitment, because Steve hasn't finished talking. He is still thinking out loud and running some things past his dad.

Son: "I've outlined my course and what it will cost. Here are some figures."

Dad could interrupt and say: "Well, the figures speak for themselves. Not much of a problem making that decision" (because dad wants Steve to sell his car anyway). But dad resists the urge and instead says: "A mature way to approach the problem." He is still waiting for Steve to make his own decision about the matter.

Steve knows dad is interested, not biased. He knows dad appreciates his point of view and gives him credit for having good judgment. Dad will not voice an opinion until asked and then might say: "Steve, how do *you* feel about it? You obviously have put in a lot of time and effort studying both sides."

Ben came home from work at the supermarket, having been fired when they cut down because of a sales slump.

"Well, you can't expect them to keep you on if it costs them money, can you?" dad might have said. "You're a luxury they can't afford."

Or mom could have said, "Well, you'll get another job."

Both of these statements may be true, but they are of no concern to Ben at the moment. And they certainly do not reflect any understanding of his immediate concern—the way he feels about having lost a job. Let's try it again.

Mom: "You enjoyed that job, didn't you?"

Ben: "Yes. I liked the hours, and it helped with school expenses."

Dad was about to say, "I'll get you another job." Instead he said, "You liked the people you worked with too, didn't you?"

Ben: "Yeah, I sure did. Guess I'll get busy and look for another job."

Ben knew that his parents were listening. They sensed the importance of the job to him, the hurt at losing it, and they didn't minimize the loss. They were allowing him to work out the problem himself, which he felt capable of doing.

Ben went on his way feeling better about the loss of his job and knowing he had some understanding parents. And he had confidence that *he* could find another job.

Carol couldn't feel lower. She does not have a date for the big spring dance and knows it is getting too late to be asked. "Boys. They're terrible! They leave you hanging and hoping. They're a bunch of creeps, anyway. I wouldn't go with one if he did ask me!"

Mom knew that Carol had not treated some of her boyfriends as well as she should have. They had asked her to school games that she didn't particularly want to see. She didn't care for sports that much.

She had other things *she* wanted to do. She hadn't gone out of her way for them, and it appeared that they were reciprocating in kind.

Mom could have said: "It's no wonder you don't have a date, the way you treat boys. You don't deserve a date." But mom was smarter than that. She knew that Carol was already aware of how she had treated the boys. She didn't need anyone (especially her mom) to remind her.

Mom just listened.

"They make you feel about that big," Carol said as she measured a quarter-inch between her fingers. "I've never felt so humiliated in my life!"

As Carol's tears started to come, mom said: "Want to talk about it?"

Of course Carol wanted to talk about it—*now*. And talk about it they did, with mom doing 99 percent of the listening.

A century ago it was common to give a sick person a bloodletting either by drawing off the blood with a leech or by actually cutting a vein and letting some of the blood escape. Unfortunately, no one was cured by this method. Those who survived did so in spite of not because of the bloodletting.

What most of them should have had was a blood transfusion to build up their reserve and increase their ability to cope with the illness. At this critical moment they needed to acquire additional strength, not to be deprived of what little strength they had left.

When our children are hurting, they need comfort. When they are struggling under a load of worry, embarrassment, humiliation, or loss of self-esteem, they certainly don't need the additional burden of disapproval or castigation from us.

What they really need is empathy, support, a listening, compassionate ear, and an understanding heart. They need a transfusion, not a bloodletting.

Samuel Augustus Maverick was a prominent Texas pioneer, statesman, and lawyer in the 1800s. He never was a cattleman, and so with some reluctance, he accepted four hundred head of cattle in payment of a debt.

With characteristic indifference, he refused to brand his cattle. When they strayed into other herds, the other ranchers called them "mavericks"; and the title has been used to designate unmarked stray cattle ever since.

Somehow I think the lost sheep of which the Savior spoke may have been mavericks of a sort. For whatever reason these sheep had not received the Savior's brand, yet the Master knew that they were missing and belonged in his fold.

Perhaps it is not appropriate to speak of the parable of the lost maverick, but look around you. There are a lot of lost mavericks among us, and many of them are young ones. Somewhere along the line they did not receive the Savior's brand, yet they are just as much his as we are.

If truly given an opportunity, many of these mavericks would "anxiously engage" in his service if they knew the joy it could bring them. There are others who have the Savior's brand upon them through baptism, but they have forgotten that they belong to his fold.

There is only one letter difference between rustler and hustler. As parents, our hustle must be more effective than the rustle of those who would draw these mavericks away from the fold.

And our hustle will be most attractive if it convinces them that they are wanted, loved, and that they belong. We can recognize their right to be mavericks, to think differently and to choose different paths. But we can also let them know how we feel about them.

My parents had ten children, and I recall how carefully they checked to see that all of us were in at night before they closed their eyes. I don't recall their having said: "Well, we have 80 percent of them in. Let's rest on the average and call it a day." They were more likely to say: "We still have two unaccounted for. We dare not rest until we find them."

Although children often object to our checking on them so carefully, they need to know that we do care enough to be concerned and that we will not rest until they, whether mavericks or not, are safely in the fold.

The time comes when your son or daughter wants to get married—soon, that is. In your eyes it may be *too* soon. But are you sure it is not the right course? What will you do about it?

Consider the case of Roy and Judy. They walked, but their feet didn't touch the ground. Roy and Judy were walking on air. One look at the glow on their faces immediately tattled what had happened—a proposal, an acceptance.

Now they were on their way to tell Judy's parents. And naturally they expected their parents to be as enthusiastic as they were. At twenty, Roy still had two more years of college, and at nineteen, Judy had completed just one year at the university.

For years now, Judy's folks had talked of nothing but a college education for all of their children—particularly Judy, their eldest. Roy's parents, on the other hand, had agreed to help him through school *if* he didn't get married. Of this agreement they had constantly reminded him.

Enthusiasm was quickly chilled by the parents on both sides, but this obstacle only served to increase their determination to get married. As arguments became more heated, minds became more fixed. Because the entire problem was becoming less solvable, the bishop was called to counsel.

In his wisdom, the bishop soon established several pertinent facts. First of all, both Roy and Judy were worthy to go to the temple to be married. Second, they were not only anxious but insistent upon *temple* marriage. Third, although it would mean that Judy would have to give up school for the present, she was qualified for secretarial work and could help put Roy through school. Roy could work part-time, and both seemed confident that they could make a go of things financially.

Although the young folks had maintained their virtue, they both recognized the fact that their emotions were reaching a dangerous level. For a year they had dated—steady for the last six months. Their likes, their dislikes, their interests, their goals, seemed to be in the same direction.

This couple had reached the point at which they had only three choices:

1. Break up. This they absolutely refused to do because they felt positive of their love for each other.

2. Continue to date and run the risk of going too far. Fortunately they had recognized this for what it was, and they wanted to avoid it.

3. Get married. This they had planned to do, they hoped with their parents' blessings, in the temple, starting off on the right foot with their marriage.

For the parents the problem seemed to boil down to two objections:

1. Fear that Judy would not get her education.

2. Fear that because of economic obstacles, Roy would not be able to finish his schooling.

In many cases the parents are unable to offer financial assistance to young people. Admittedly many young marriages go on the rocks. But after considerable interviewing and patient listening, the bishop was able to counsel the parents on both sides that he felt these young people *should* get married *now*.

"If these young people are forced to defer marriage, both families may have great cause for regret. It might take a little sacrifice on the part of everyone. Judy would have to put off her schooling for a while. Roy and Judy will have to skimp by on a rather anemic budget.

"Both families might have to contribute some financial help, even in the form of a loan. But when two young people are in love, when they seem suited to each other, when they are worthy, and when they want to go to the temple, some of the plans of parents for their children have to be changed. To do otherwise may cause a loss of virtue and worthiness, a forced marriage, and a faulty beginning to a relationship that otherwise could have been so perfect."

Of course, there are bound to be other factors. In some cases one or the other is not a member of the Church. One or the other may not be worthy to go to the temple. Of one thing you may be sure, however, when the couple is ready and determined to marry, deferring the marriage for various reasons may be extremely hazardous.

This is most certainly not to say that teenage marriages should be condoned or encouraged. But if parents are to avoid heartache, they must be realistic. In spite of their youth, these young people are physiologically endowed with powerful hormones that may be difficult to control. These young people are intelligent enough to recognize when they are nearing dangerous ground. When they are honorable enough to come to their parents and to lay the problem before them, their integrity should be honored by a fair, interested, and compassionate hearing.

If marriage seems the only acceptable plan, then parents should give the children their blessing and allow them to begin this new relationship with a good feeling. One of the unforgettable sins is failure to accept a new son or daughter at first or to accept them with reservations. Even though attempts are made to make amends later on, the damage and the hurt have been done.

Lastly, both the parents and the bishop will do well to develop good listening ears, attentive, compassionate, understanding ears that will hear these young people out. During such a listening session, the young people might even talk themselves into waiting for marriage as they verbalize the pros and cons of marriage and its many responsibilities.

On the other hand, such a discussion may show that the two young people are very discerning. Perhaps they have thought things out pretty well. Maybe they do have a good case. Possibly they *should* get married—and *now*. But either way, parents, don't deny them your blessing.

Virginia is twenty, a sophomore in college, has just under a four-point average and is in love.* George is twenty-four, a senior soon to graduate, has served a mission in England, and wants Virginia to marry him—*now*.

If they marry, Virginia likely will not finish college because George wants to get his master's degree and follow it with a doctorate. Although George is intelligent, he is no scholar. Of the two, Virginia has by far the greater potential.

What should she do?

Virginia has mixed feelings about the ambivalent roles a woman must play. She knows that it is not good for man to be alone, but she also knows that it is not good for woman to be alone either. Only too well she foresees a career of success and achievement for herself, for she has always reached and surpassed any goal she has set for her-

---

*Adapted from *Living, Loving and Marrying*, by Lindsay R. Curtis and Wayne J. Anderson, Salt Lake City: Publishers Press, 1968.

self. She is well aware that she could possibly outearn George, whose pride would be sorely wounded if she did.

Yet Virginia is perceptive enough to realize that while love ofttimes knocks at the door more than once, it may tire of the waiting and depart, never to return again. Spinsterhood stands as a stark specter before every woman who turns down love. And she does love George—of this much she is certain.

One cannot generalize because personalities and situations vary, but one must be aware of the pitfalls in either case. How does the potential husband feel about his wife's working? Will he insist upon being the only breadwinner, even though a poor one? Does the future bride dislike the role of housekeeping and motherhood so intensely that she insists upon working outside the home? Can she really enjoy the role of wife and mother in the home?

What about Virginia's leaving school? Is she going to resent George because he prevented her from graduating? Is she going to wonder how far she might have gone in her own career?

Of course, one cannot really answer these questions. One can only speculate. But who is to say that Virginia cannot help George complete his education, have her family, and then return to school and complete requirements for a degree?

Nor is there a pat answer to the question: Should a mother work outside the home? The widowed or divorced woman raising a family will probably have to for economic reasons. Need too will sometimes dictate this even in two-parent homes. With home and children well organized, many of these women can adequately fill the dual role of managing a home and children and also working at a job, and as the children assume more responsibility they may well become better disciplined and more competent and confident persons.

In the case of Virginia and George, they were too much in love to break up their relationship. Both were aware that the time had come when the only alternative to this was to get married.

So married they were, and Virginia started to work to put George through the rest of his training. As so often happens, they had not planned on additions to their family, but these came anyway.

George is now taking somewhat longer to complete his studies because he is working on the side, but they are managing all right. In fact, Virginia is now expecting her second child.

It is not to be implied that every couple should get married when the idea strikes them. But young people do have a way of working things out that often amazes both peers and parents. At times their resourcefulness draws strength from invisible sources.

When two young people demonstrate maturity by recognizing that their relationship is becoming too intimate, they should be encouraged to marry and not to wait. They should not be forced to tempt fate and their own seething, youthful emotions beyond their capacity to withstand them. When given the opportunity, these young people will outperform our greatest expectations.

Let's wish them well in marriage and give them our blessing.

One of the great arts we as parents are required to perfect is the ability to convey to our children our concern, our love, and our interest, without taking away from them their individuality, their ego, their self-esteem, or their priceless free agency. We will not achieve this expertise overnight, nor does the Lord expect us to. But with his help and with constant effort, we can become skilled parents, lovingly wise in our dealings with the children who have been entrusted to our care.

CHAPTER FIVE

A FEW GUIDELINES

In dealing with young people and their problems, we need to master a few techniques. One is to back off.

There is a difference between backing off and giving up. I recall a home in which we lived that had huge floor-to-ceiling glass on each end. How we enjoyed the light that permeated the house because of these huge walls of glass! Anyone standing outside the house could see completely through the house from one end to the other.

But this very unique view through our home was puzzling to a certain bird. For almost the entire time we lived in that house (three years) we received a daily visit from an angry, bewildered bird who thought he should be able to fly through the house from one end to the other, simply because he could see through the house. When we heard a pecking against the glass, we knew this bird had come for one of his frequent angry and frustrating visits.

He began pecking at one pane, then angrily flew against the next pane, and the next, until he had finally spent his wrath against each pane of glass. His visit was concluded by pecking ferociously against the last panel of glass before he gave up and flew away in bewildered defeat.

Somehow I think even a birdbrain would know when to back off and admit that such a flight through the house, at least for the present, was impossible. How many times, I wondered, does that bird have to test the glass to prove to himself that it is impenetrable?

Yet how often do we as parents peck away (at times angrily) at our children over some problem from which we should, for the present at least, back away—not give up perhaps—but at least back off.

Some years ago one of my sons confided that he would be delighted to accompany me on a short trip if I wouldn't (as always) lecture to him. If I had used just a part of this same worn-out and senseless lecturing energy to understand and to *listen* to him, just imagine what a pleasant and rewarding time we might have enjoyed together! I hadn't learned when to back off.

Instead of pecking away at him and becoming frustrated, I should have realized that such lecturing merely causes irritation and resentment. There is a distinct difference between backing off and giving up. Back off but never give up!

Now consider the matter of privileges and rights.

Privileges quickly come to be taken for granted and soon are counted as *rights* by young and old alike. By the second or third encounter, privileges are no longer looked upon as rights but as demands. The best safeguard against such evolution is to grant privileges based upon performance.

"Yes, Jan," said mom, "not only may you go to the dance, but I will press your dress and help you get ready. But first you must clean your room as you were asked to do."

Jan: "I'll do it when I get home. I don't have time right now because I have to go over and see Jill first."

Mom: "Your permission to go to the dance will come after the room has been cleaned, and I can't begin pressing your dress until you begin cleaning your room."

Discussion closed. Refuse to argue or debate the case. Just go about your other tasks. Whenever a parent begins to argue with a child, it means that the subject is still open to negotiation, the child can still get his own way. Too often a privilege becomes a right and a right develops into a demand—without one's having paid the price.

On one occasion I asked a group of young people what they would change in their parents if they had the opportunity to do so. One answered that he wished his parents would set some definite rules. He would abide by such rules. "The way it is now," he said, "I never am sure where I stand or how far I can go with their approval."

They left everything up to him. They "trusted" him. But he would have appreciated more definite boundaries. He wanted his parents to care more about what he did. Their confidence he already had. But parameters of performance issued by them would not only have been appreciated but also would have shown that they cared.

Repetition is monotonous to the hearer. One of the sure signs of approaching senility is the tendency to repeat oneself. But this problem is not always restricted to the senile. It seems to appear as soon as one becomes a parent.

"How many times have I told you *not* to leave your clothes on the floor?" Or, "How many times do I have to tell you to pick up your room?" "I've told you a thousand times not to do that!"

Perhaps if we had said it once, clearly, with an unmistakable explanation of what would happen if the child did or did not do as he was told, the warning wouldn't have to be repeated. And punishment would be expected and received by the disobedient child.

Someone has said that those alcoholics who continue to be alcoholics are the ones who know their spouses don't mean what they say when they threaten them. This could also apply to children. They soon learn whether we voice only empty threats.

How futile to threaten when we *know* we won't carry out the threat! How foolish to threaten things that are unreasonable!

If we threaten to cut off a child's allowance if he disobeys, we must be certain we can carry it out. Remember, there are certain things we can't cut off, such a school lunch money, school fees, and so forth.

The use of cars can be cut off, but we must reckon with the fact that our child has a friend with a car. When restricting a child's activities, we should remember that there are certain required appointments and commitments. In other words, we had better think before we threaten.

Most wife beaters could quickly be cured if the wife would say after the first beating, "Once more and I leave!" and mean it. If a child speaks disrespectfully, if he consistently disobeys, it could be because we have tolerated such behavior all along. Monotony of repetition can be avoided if we mean what we say.

What time do we expect our children to be in? Do we expect them to call us if they will be unavoidably late? Do we inquire where they are going? Do we know anything about their companion, his driving habits, or his standards? Our son or daughter can probably fill us in on these important issues without an inquisition. But we should do it before the companion arrives on the scene. Let's avoid embarrassment or confrontation in the presence of others. Preserve our children's self-esteem. We can ask questions that show that we care.

Fence lines do not take away freedom. Let me illustrate. An infant or toddler does not know the difference between sidewalk and street. For his own safety and freedom to wander about without a leash, he is placed within a playpen, then perhaps graduated to a fenced-in yard.

Children, if turned loose on an unfenced playground, will generally play only in the center of the field. By contrast, if there is a high protective fence surrounding the playground they will run freely and explore every corner—perhaps even running against the fence to test it—because they know that they are safe within the confines of that fence.

To make the best use of water, we build up levees to control rivers and build dams in which to store that water. Without safe levees along rivers, the adjoining property can quickly turn to swamp land.

Children want freedom, but usually they want safety along with the freedom. That is the reason why they want some fence lines, and they want us to walk those fence lines with them to be sure we care about them.

We do not have to apologize for rules and regulations in our society. Rules provide order instead of chaos. Without them we might become like a river that follows the line of least resistance—crooked and without principle or discipline.

Naturally the question comes up as to where to place the limits. How far is too far? How late is too late? Parents must decide this for themselves, then discuss it with their son or daughter before the companion arrives.

Keep in mind that if we squeeze the sponge too tightly, we will squeeze all of the water out of it. We want our children to absorb all of the self-confidence, self-esteem, and trust they can. If we squeeze the sponge too tightly, however, and are too restrictive, we will destroy all three of these noble qualities.

We can give our children a full vote of confidence as we walk the fence line with them.

Young people are a lot like willows. Willows vary not only in size but also in pliability. Some are so pliable they can be woven into the most intricate of designs. Others, called "crack" willows, are more brittle and may break when subjected to a severe wind. Each willow must be handled differently according to its pliability.

Our children are much the same as willows. Some we can almost wrap around our finger, while others are less pliable and break if subjected to any rigorous bending of their ways. Obviously children cannot all be treated alike.

Wise parents study their children and learn as they are growing up just how best to counsel with them and direct them. As we study them, we learn how pliable they are, how far they may bend without breaking.

Everything needs room to grow. I can recall a row of poplar trees that my dad planted in front of our old home when I was just a boy. Because these young trees were brittle and easily broken off by the wind or by boys passing by, dad decided they would require some kind of special protection.

Knowing that too much restriction might hamper their growth yet knowing that they needed some safeguard, my dad devised an interesting plan. A strong wooden stake was pounded into the ground alongside each sapling to give it stability.

But now the problem arose: How should the young tree be anchored to the stake? A chain would chafe and scar the bark of such a small tree. A rope would wear through as the tree swayed in the breeze. A wire would soon cut through to the heart of the tree.

Finally a loop of garden hose was placed loosely around the trunk of the tree and anchored to the stake. This permitted freedom for the sapling to sway with the breeze, without chafing. Yet the garden hose protected it from destruction by a severe wind or wayward vandals.

Our children likewise need support. They need a certain amount of protection. But they must not be stifled by strangulating restrictions that do not allow them sufficient freedom to grow and develop, to move around.

Let's give them some rules. Let's give them reasonable, sensible limits within which they can move about and feel comfortable, and within which they can grow and can grow straight. After they become sufficiently strong (and straight) they can discard the collar of containment and continue to grow on their own.

And how about prejudging our youth? Let me give an analogy.

Just outside the big bay windows of our cabin in the pines we have prepared in full view, on top of an old stump, an eye-level platform. On this miniature stage chipmunks, squirrels, and occasionally birds and even mice provide a continuous entertainment before the entranced gaze of our many grandchildren.

As an enticement to these curious creatures we place heaps of rolled oats in plenteous piles. What fun it is to hear the squirrels chide and cajole us as soon as we arrive at the cabin, impatiently waiting for us to spread their bounteous breakfast before them! We imagine countless other tiny eyes peering at us from the shadows and anxiously awaiting their regular handout.

The larger animals usually take their turn first. Immediately after they have filled their jowls, these actors are replaced by smaller ones, in their own specific pecking order. Mice, it seems, must wait for their turn until after dark when the other animals are comfortably tucked away.

As we watched these animals enjoy their generous honorarium of oats and applause, we wondered if perhaps we might be doing them a disservice. Were we depriving them of the fun, the work, and the experience of scrounging for themselves to obtain their food? Could this generous gesture even make them incapable of fending for themselves after we were gone?

An even more serious question arose in our minds. Would this kindness on our part prevent them from storing up their winter supplies and thus leave them victims of mid-winter starvation?

As the chipmunks and squirrels gorged themselves, they reminded us of teenagers at a pie-eating contest. Ravenously they crammed their cheeks with food until their little jowls could hold no more. Like starved adolescents, they wolfed their food. Our concern about the winter months mounted. What would they do when we closed everything down at the end of the summer? Would it be too late to store for winter?

We had truly misjudged them. They did not swallow that food—quite the contrary. As soon as their jowls were bulging, they scurried to their burrow to meticulously stack this food on their winter storage pile. Promptly they hurried back to the heap of oats to refill the only "pockets" nature had given them.

We learned a lesson from these tireless troopers.

How often we make premature judgment of our fellowmen and especially our teenagers before we have all the facts! How often we criticize severely and unjustly because of what we *think* they might or might not be doing.

When all the evidence is in, the facts so often vindicate these young folks, just as they did for the chattering chipmunks and the scampering squirrels.

Some of you may recall the Brigham Young University versus Southern Methodist University football game in which BYU came from behind in the last few minutes of the exciting game and won a once-in-a-lifetime cliff-hanger. A few of my friends became disgusted with BYU early in the game and switched over to another channel. Some even went to bed early in the game, fully disenchanted and convinced that BYU had been mismatched. They couldn't stand to watch the anticipated result. Actually these sports fans missed the most spectacular, exciting come-from-behind win in that school's entire history—all because they prejudged and categorized the game before the final score was in.

As parents we are often guilty, in varying degrees, of prejudging our children and young people in general. We are prone to leave the game before it is over, to write off some child as a failure because of a

53

poor start. We too often say: "I *expected* such a poor showing. He won't (or can't) change anyway."

The only time a person can't change is when he is no longer alive. Even then he changes back into dust. We should never concede the game until the final score has been posted, especially when dealing with our children.

Joel, age nine, had never been interested in reading books. He preferred to watch television or engage in almost any physical activity. After starting school he had become irritable at home and combative on the playground.

His teacher reported that he was lazy and inattentive. In the first grade he was labeled "lazy" and possibly "retarded." His peers called him stupid and dumb. It remained for his alert second grade teacher to determine that Joel had dyslexia. Small wonder that he became frustrated and angry!

There was nothing wrong with Joel's mind. He simply could not read because words appeared backward to him.

Occasionally children develop similar symptoms because of impaired eyesight, a problem that usually can be corrected with eyeglasses. Other children have one "lazy" eye, an eye whose muscles do not keep it in focus with the other eye, thus giving them double vision. This is also correctable.

What I am saying is that we should look for the cause of behavioral problems rather than at the erratic behavior. Stress in the family, parental quarrels, threatened divorce, insecurity of various causes and types—all of these can provoke unacceptable behavior and waywardness as a form of rebellion against what is happening to the child.

Young girls often get married just to escape intolerable conditions at home. Boys run away from home to escape a domineering father only to find themselves unable to cope with the world except by crime and criminal associations. Such a boy is usually labeled the "wayward son."

Those of us whose stewardship involves young people should look for the special girl or boy who is having problems. Perhaps we should also look for the one who is a problem and ask ourselves why he is a problem. More than discipline, he may need understanding. Instead of punishment, he may require help in solving his situation.

If a youth's attitudes and activities reach the point of making life a misery for the rest of the family, the solution may be the tough one.

Ed was forty-one, successful in business, respected in the community and church, father of four children, and husband of an attractive, vivacious wife. The future looked good, except for Paul, Ed's sixteen-year-old son.

Until six months ago Paul had been a quiet, studious, obedient, and delightful son. Then at school Paul became acquainted with Doug, who not only had accepted Paul but also had introduced him to a group of three other boys who associated with each other.

Almost from the beginning of this friendship Paul's grades had suffered and his attitude toward school, family, and life in general had changed. He was no longer the boy he had been. His hair had always been well groomed yet stylish. Now it was unkempt and uncombed. Instead of a daily shower, it was questionable if he ever bathed.

His clothes became soiled and began to smell bad just as Paul himself did. It was obvious that he had taken up smoking, and Ed also suspected he was using drugs. Paul flouted beer cans, even placing a six-pack in the refrigerator as a "challenge" to his parents. Things were reaching a breaking point.

As Paul's behavior changed, so did his dad's. Ed at first felt hurt and disappointed. Gradually Ed became angered at Paul's appearance as well as his behavior. It was embarrassing to Ed and to his family and friends.

Perhaps worst of all, Ed was frustrated at his own inability to cope with the situation. The more he became frustrated, the louder he shouted and the more abusive his language became. He was unhappy with Paul, but he was also unhappy with himself and his inability to cope with such a dilemma.

Ed had always been able to handle anything that came up in his business or in his home. He was basically a loving, understanding father and a devoted husband. Now he was finding it difficult to be any of these.

What can one do in such a situation? How far must a parent go or allow a child to go before deciding: This is far enough!

Every situation is different. Every child is different. But a family is a family, and husband and wife are entitled to a happy bond of marriage. In short, no child has the right to destroy a family or a marriage.

But before Ed can regain control of the situation, he must first regain control of himself. Nothing is ever solved in anger. And he and his wife must present a unified front, a strong marriage.

Ed must also realize that he may not be able to change his son— at least not at this point. But in the meantime Ed must prevent Paul from destroying the family and his marriage.

Choosing an appropriate time Ed called Paul into his study and closed the door. "Son, what are your plans?"

Paul: "What do you mean?"

Dad: "What are your plans for the future?"

Paul: "I don't have any. I just want to be left alone—not lectured to or shouted at."

Dad: "Well, as you know, things have not been very pleasant around here lately for any of us."

Paul: "Yeah, and I suppose you are going to say it's all my fault."

Dad was tempted to take off on another big argument and shouting match, but he had carefully thought this out and decided that there was to be no shouting or argument.

Dad: "If you have any plans I want you to know that I am willing to listen."

Paul: "I told you I don't have any."

Dad: "Then perhaps you won't mind if I tell you of our plans."

Paul: "Here goes a lecture again; okay, which lecture this time?"

Dad again was tempted to say some pretty harsh things, but he resisted.

Dad: "Mom and I love each other very much. We love each of you children more than we can express. We value our family above anything else in the world."

Paul no longer looked his dad in the face. He no longer challenged him. He stared at the floor. He knew in his heart all of this was true.

Dad: "Because we love all of you so much and because we value our family so much, we are not willing to let anything or anyone destroy it. And because I love your mother so much, I am willing to defend our marriage against anything and anybody.''

Ed did not raise his voice, but found it difficult to keep the emotions back as he spoke of his love for his family.

Dad: ''Paul, perhaps you are not aware of what you have been doing.''

Paul: ''Here we go.''

Dad: ''I don't think you are aware of what you have been doing to our family. The love that we have always had for each other has suffered. We have had arguments and unkind words that never found their way into this home before. At times I even found myself speaking unkind words to your mother.''

Paul: ''I suppose you blame me.''

Dad: ''It is not a case of blame. It is a case of behavior. Your behavior simply does not belong in our way of life. We have standards in this family, and these standards have always brought happiness to us. They have fostered a feeling of love and serenity in this home.

''What I am really saying is that we can no longer tolerate your type of behavior because it threatens to destroy our family and the love that we have in our home.

''There are a couple of things neither one of us can change. First of all, you are our son. We can't change that, and I want you to know that I wouldn't change it if I could.

''The second thing is that we love you. We may not approve of what you are doing, but we love you and always will.

''But you must change if you are to remain a member of this household. You know that you have your free agency. You are free to do as you please. But if you are to remain a member of this family, there are some things that you must change.

''We have three other children to consider as well as your mother and myself. We want you to be a member of the family, a happy member. But we will not permit you or anyone else to destroy us.

''Now, Paul, with sincere love in my heart, I am prepared to listen to your plans for the future.''

There are those of us who might accuse Ed of ''throwing out his son," of "abandoning" him when he most needs help. Quite the contrary. Ed is not throwing out his son or abandoning him.

If Ed permits Paul to continue as he is now doing, he will be abandoning him to destruction by drugs and a probable life of crime to sustain them. Ed is doing what he probably should have done before now. He is laying it on the line with his son, without argument, without shouting, but without compromising. And he is doing it not with vindictiveness but with love and a desire to have his son remain in the family.

Perhaps most important of all right now is consistency. Ed must stick to his guns and not equivocate. He can offer help to Paul if he is willing to change. If he is not willing to change, then Paul must leave the home so as not to destroy it. It is Paul's decision now.

Because Paul has always been able to stir up a scene, to foster a nasty argument and bad words, he has always been in control. For the first time Paul's dad is in full control, and Paul knows that his dad means business. Paul must change or lose everything. And it is better for him to make that decision now, before drugs destroy his brain and dull his senses.

If Paul decides to leave, as he may well threaten to do, mom and dad must withstand the hurt and realize that what they are doing must be done. If Paul indeed does leave, it is likely he will come back. In any event, mom and dad will have a better chance for success with the rest of their family.

Many Pauls have changed their ways and done a turnabout. A few have persisted in the wrong direction; however, this also may be temporary. Certainly Ed did all he could do, and he did it in love.

Ed really attacked the problem rather than the person. He made it clear that they loved the person (Paul) but not what his behavior was doing to the family. Paul would not respect his dad if he didn't stand up for the family.

In dealing with misbehavior, focus may be all-important. By adjusting it, you can take the heat off a hot situation.

Try a simple experiment the next time you bathe or shower. As you raise a leg to dry it, focus your attention on the one leg upon which you are standing and on the possibility that you might lose your balance. You guessed it, you very likely will lose your balance and have to support yourself.

On the other hand, if you focus your attention upon the leg you are drying with the towel, your automatic sense of balance takes over and makes any adjustments necessary to maintain your balance. Without thinking about the problem, your automatic pilot takes over and does the job for you.

If we constantly focus our attention upon a child's misbehavior, we are likely to lose our perspective (and equilibrium) in other areas that are also important. And we may cause the child to lose his perspective also.

Take the heat off, so to speak. Focus your attention on something else, especially a few things your child is doing right. Back off. You may be delighted at how different things look and how they often have a way of working themselves out when we give them a chance.

Keep in mind the man who insisted on uncovering every twig, pleasant or unpleasant, about the family tree. About all he uncovered were a lot of ''saps.'' Know when enough is enough, and spare your child an inquisition.

Sooner or later the child will run into an emergency that will become your emergency. Are you ready for it? What do you carry in your emergency kit?

In our cars most of us carry a tow cable and some jump cables to be used to help a neighbor whose car is stuck or whose car battery is dead. Occasionally these same cables can come in handy to help us out if *our* car is stalled.

What kind of cables do we carry in our hearts to help out our children when they are stalled by misconduct or faulty thinking? Perhaps the child needs to have his spiritual battery recharged, or he may need a temporary boost from our spiritual battery when his has gone dead. We may occasionally have to help pull him out of a sticky situation.

A sixteen-year-old was in an accident and phoned his dad to tell him about wrecking the family car. The father could have yelled at the boy, verbally chastising him in front of his friends or the police.

But the dad's first words were: "Are you all right? Is anyone hurt?" After being reassured that no one was hurt he said: "We can repair cars, but we can't always restore human bodies. We'll take a good look at things and see what we can do." Do you think that son was proud to have a father of that caliber?

Let's carry a spiritual tow cable and some compassionate jump cables in our personal emergency kit to help our children when they are in trouble. Such help will also strengthen the bond of love between us.

My next suggestion is not easy to implement, but it is important: Have the courage to let your children learn by experience.

Mammoth Cave near Louisville, Kentucky, is one of the truly spectacular sights in the world. Visitors inside the cave may explore 175 miles of underground corridors, see eight waterfalls, two lakes, and three rivers, one of which is sixty feet wide.

As visitors descend as far as 360 feet below the surface, they see in the various cave formations, shapes like trees, flowers, fruits, and waterfalls—all of these in a kaleidoscope of color.

One of the unusual wonders of the cave, however, is its strange live fish without eyes. These fish are not only blind but also have no pigment in their skin. Visitors can see through the skin into the pink flesh of their bodies.

The fish in these caverns once had eyes. Through ages of disuse in the darkness of the caves, their unused eyes have been totally lost. Likewise, these fish no longer need pigment in their skin to protect them from the sunlight.

In this cave are also sightless, wingless beetles and crickets who have suffered a similar fate.

As parents we must occasionally sit by and helplessly watch as our children make mistakes in life. How we would like to shield them from these errors and influences if we could!

You will recall, however, that the divine plan provides that we be exposed to the good and the evil, pleasure and pain, that we might learn thereby. If our children were never exposed to both influences, they would never learn to choose the good from the evil. Like the blind fish, they might lose the ability to choose.

At times we can only pray for our children and hope that they have learned correct principles to help them make the right choice. As parents we must have the courage to allow them to make that choice.

A sugar beet farmer once told me that they purposely hold back on irrigation of sugar beets long enough to permit the roots to penetrate deeply into the ground in search of water. Then when the water comes in plentiful supply the beet will grow to be many times larger than if it had been given water earlier while it was still short of its potential growth.

Perhaps some of the painful experiences that we as parents have to observe in our children give them an opportunity to grow bigger in character than they otherwise might have been able to do. Perhaps they grow more substantial roots that give them stability and dependability to handle opportunities that come later in their lives.

Every parent wants his children to have the many advantages that he (the parent) did not enjoy. In our zeal to help them have these privileges, let us not take away from them the difficulties that become stepping-stones to greatness.

In our roundup of guidelines, none is more significant than the power of parental example and stability.

Our children are surrounded by heroes, usually of the wrong kind. Baseball heroes are often shown with a "cud" of chewing tobacco in their cheeks as their trademark. Football heroes appear on beer ads. Movie stars not only extol the virtues of smoking and drinking, but also portray immorality as though it were the only way of life.

Never have our children been more in need of heroes of the right kind. Sometimes we are led to believe that we, as parents, rate rather low on the child's totem pole of heroes. But when the chips are down, when a child really needs a friend, parents leave the entire crowd behind.

Parents are like life buoys that steer their children through hazardous channels of life. Life buoys, however, would be of no value whatever if they were not anchored, if they did not maintain their position, if they were not constant.

We live in an age of disposables. I recall an extremely clever instrument I once devised for my particular specialty in medicine. The surgical supply companies acknowledged its practicality and praised my ingenuity, but they would not buy it because it was not disposable. They were not anxious to have something that would last forever. They preferred something that had to be replaced with a new one after each use.

Automobiles are often bought nowadays because of their turn-in value in a year or two. No one seems to be anxious to keep a car for a long time. Youth of today have grown up with paper tissues and towels. Disposable milk cartons, cups, paper plates, and pans are the order of the day. No longer are many products made to last, but to throw away after one use.

Even in surgery we now use a knife blade only once and then throw it away. Scissors, forceps, tweezers, clamps, and other instruments are built to be thrown away. Syringes are used once and thrown away. Drapes, towels, gloves, gowns, all fit into the same category.

Somehow, though, in all this "disposable" world of ours, children expect constancy from their parents. They expect us to be like life buoys anchored to the same spot, always where they expect to find us, always standing by our standards and ideals in spite of the fact they (the children) have complained at those same standards.

To abandon such a positive, stable position would be comparable to a parent throwing a life jacket made of sugar lumps to a drowning child. Let us be examples—solid examples of stability, constancy, and character for our children regardless of time, place, or situation.

CHAPTER SIX

WHEN IT HAS ALREADY HAPPENED

S tan is twenty. In his early teens he fell in with the wrong crowd and drifted away from the Church and from the standards upheld by his family. Stan is not a failure—far from it. But he has failed to live the way his parents and the Lord would like him to live.

Every time his parents visit Stan he is on the defensive. "Wonder what they'll lecture about today," Stan says. He is torn between love and admiration for them as parents and the resentment he feels because of their unrelenting attempts to change his ways. Frequently he turns to more drinking after a visit from them.

When asked if they love him, Stan's parents are offended. "Of course we love him and want the best for him."

"Is it possible for you to love him in spite of certain habits he has and the fact that he is totally inactive in the Church?" I asked.

"Definitely we love him. *But* we certainly wish he could see the error of his ways," they say. Little do they realize that they have just placed a condition upon their love for him. Yes, they resolve not to hound him or prod him or make remarks that suggest he should repent. *But* they always manage to slip in some remark that (in Stan's mind) pours poison on their visit.

Another case. Keith was one of five children in a typical Mormon family. All of the other children were active, and Keith's two brothers had gone on missions. At age fifteen Keith took up with inactive friends and soon picked up their habits.

It wasn't long before he moved out of the home and into an apartment with his friends. His entire life changed as he took up drugs along with liquor and tobacco. Somewhere along the way virtue also walked out of the door.

Keith's parents were brokenhearted and shed many tears over the situation. Keith's long hair made it embarrassing for him to come home, and of course his clothes always smelled of tobacco. This was especially offensive to his mother.

Keith's side of the picture was that his parents brought him food and other goodies, but the main purpose of their visit was to give him a lecture, one which he had heard many times.

Keith's parents came to see me about this and sobbed pitifully as they described Keith's rapidly deteriorating condition. For over an hour I listened, all the while praying that I might be able to give them some comfort as well as wise counsel.

As I listened for the Spirit and inspiration, I was somewhat surprised at the question I was prompted to ask them. "Do you folks *truly* love Keith?" They were justifiably offended at the question. Would they have come for counsel had they not loved him? Couldn't I sense the sincere sorrow on their faces?

"Let me rephrase that question," I said. "Do you love Keith without reservation? Can you love him the way he is, the way he now lives? Can you love him *in spite* of what he has done and is doing to you?"

"Yes. *But* we know that this is not good for him, and we know where it will eventually lead. How can we help him to change?"

"Stop trying so hard to change him. May I simply suggest that you go to visit him with only one thing on your minds and in your hearts—*love* for him, unqualified love. Let him see in your eyes that you love him. Even if you say nothing at all. Just love him. And let's see what happens."

Shortly after this Keith did a complete turnaround. He cut his hair and he showed up at the ward where I was bishop. As he became more and more active in the ward, he and I developed a close friendship.

When the time was right, I asked Keith a question. "What influenced you to change your life; to give up drugs and other habits;

and to make that difficult decision to leave your friends, straighten out your life and come back to church?"

"Bishop," said Keith, "one day my parents came to see me and they looked different. For the first time they didn't snoop around and sniff to see what and if I had been smoking. They didn't look at my long hair with that typical disapproving expression. They didn't ask about the drugs. And they didn't prod me to go to church. In fact, I don't believe they said anything. But for the first time in a long while I could see *love* in their eyes. I *knew* that they loved me."

Love is more powerful than we think. And frequently it is the only power we have left.

Resist the urge to preach, to counsel, to admonish. Listen with love in your heart. You may find the most inspiring visit is one in which you say nothing and do nothing but listen with empathy. Your son and daughter will know and feel that you love them.

You may have heard of "memory plastics." Plastics in general are easily molded or changed in shape by pressure. In this modern day of plastics there are so many different types of plastics that they can simulate almost any other substance such as leather, silk, cotton, wool, metal, wood, or even rubber.

Progress in the field of plastics is so rapid that it changes almost from day to day, as new and exciting combinations and inventions are added.

One very interesting plastic, for example, is one whose molecules "remember" the shape of the article which they form. A hairbrush handle, for instance, can be made of memory plastic. The same hairbrush handle can then be heated and drawn into a long, thin rod of plastic.

But when this piece of plastic is reheated, its molecules remember their molecular "arrangement" as a hairbrush handle and form themselves once more into the same shape. As you can imagine, this memory plastic finds countless uses, one of which is to "shrink" tight-fitting pieces of plastic together.

Children have some of these same qualities. Shawn first began to change his shape at about age fourteen. By the age of twenty he had been "drawn" into an ungainly image that his parents have not been able to accept. But who is to say that someone won't come along who will put his arm around Shawn, warm him up, and cause his molecules to "rearrange" themselves to form the image that he once was.

Deep down inside, Shawn has not forgotten the shape he once had. The difficult part for Shawn's parents is to develop the patience it takes to see one of their children doing things he shouldn't do and still retain the hope that he someday can and will change.

Another case. Tom is now twenty-nine. He also made a wrong turn at about age fifteen and has kept the same company and way of life ever since. His father is a most successful professional man who could and would offer Tom every opportunity to follow in his footsteps or obtain an education in any field.

Alas, Tom is a high school dropout and has no intention of going back to school. But even without his schooling, Tom is a master mechanic. He is a "natural." He can fix almost anything mechanical. Instead of frowning on Tom's inclination toward a mechanic's trade and nagging him toward a professional career, which Tom does not want, his dad has maintained an excellent close contact with him. At the present time, dad is helping him acquire the necessary quality tools for his trade and is justly proud of Tom.

Tom receives no lectures from his dad. He already knows that his dad would help him with an education. But they settled that issue long ago. Tom needs to be accepted and loved, *now,* as is. And that is exactly what his dad is providing. Mom has a little more problem accepting this so-called comedown from what he "could be," but she is gradually adjusting.

Tom's dad takes him to lunch frequently and brags him up to his colleagues as the best mechanic he has ever known. In his dad's eyes, Tom is not a failure merely because he failed to choose the same white-collar profession that his dad has.

At the present time Tom is not active or even friendly toward the Church, even though his parents are extremely active. They have not allowed Tom's inactivity in Church to interfere with their close relationship. The "memory plastic" in this case has not found sufficient warmth of the proper type yet to cause Tom to revert back to the "hairbrush handle" he was first molded to be. But in the meantime, Tom and his dad are great pals, each respecting the other's rights and behavior.

Another case. Larry, age twenty-five, grew up in a marvelous religious environment, his father having served as bishop and also as stake president. Both Larry and his brother served honorable missions. Larry's brother has gone on to become a bishop himself and to hold countless other offices in the Church. He and his wife and children all participate in Church activities.

For some reason after Larry returned from his mission, he turned away from the Church and took up the typical habits of the inactive. This caused considerable sorrow in both of Larry's parents. But these noble, prominent parents have continued to love Larry without criticism, without lecturing, and without rehearsing his faults to him. Larry still feels their love, and he feels comfortable around them because they make him feel comfortable.

The avenues of communication are still open. Though married to an inactive Mormon wife, Larry's door is still wide open to his parents because of their noncritical attitude. As I have observed this family, I have the feeling that something good will happen. Someone will come along that will "reheat" the molecules in Larry's make-up and cause them to rearrange themselves as they once were. He will again resume the image the Lord intended for him to have. But how wise these parents are to maintain his love and respect in the meantime.

Another case. Sheela feels so bad about the inactivity of her married son, Bert, that she weeps every time she is around him or thinks about him. Can you imagine how uncomfortable this makes Bert feel? He is reminded constantly that he is a disappointment to his parents (especially to his mother), and he can never find any joy in their presence. Why should he want to come to see them or have them come to see him if such a meeting is always accompanied by tears?

And Sheela cannot resist telling Bert why she is crying. "I just can't help it when I think of all you are throwing away. And when I realize what you could be doing in the Church! Just look at your brother who is in the bishopric. . . ."

One of the reasons why I have always felt a little compassion for Laman and Lemuel in the Book of Mormon is that their well-meaning father constantly held up their younger brother Nephi as an example to them. I can see Laman and Lemuel becoming more infuriated every time they were reminded that their behavior was not as acceptable as Nephi's, "even though he is younger than you." This does not justify their behavior, but it may explain part of their rebellious attitude.

Another case. Stella and Lawrence had enjoyed a good marriage until their daughter Pam began to kick over the traces. Instead of bolstering their own relationship to withstand the disappointments that were to come, both Stella and Lawrence were so incensed and upset at Pam's behavior that they began to let her "use" them.

Soon they found themselves bickering, even pointing the finger of blame at each other for her aberrant behavior. Pam quickly discovered that she could avoid criticism and discipline directed toward her by pitting one parent against the other.

Yes, children can play one parent against the other to avoid criticism themselves, but in so doing they are destroying the very pillar of hope and the anchor in a storm for themselves.

Children do *not* have a right to destroy a marriage. And parents should realize that before they can help a child in trouble, they must first have an unshakable bond of love and cooperation between themselves. It is difficult to save a person who is drowning if your own life raft is already beginning to sink.

First, discuss your strategy together in private. Having decided what approach to take, kneel in prayer and ask for heavenly strength to work together in harmony to accomplish that which is best for your son or daughter.

Another case. Mable came into my office along with her sixteen-year-old daughter, Christine. Tears flowed freely before Mable even began to talk. "I can't believe a daughter of mine would do this to me," Mable sobbed. "I am so ashamed!"

At the time when her daughter needed a mother's support more than any other time, Mable had let her daughter down. Agreed, pregnancy out of wedlock is not exactly easy on parents, especially parents who are active in the Church and respected in the community.

But what about Christine? If a sixteen-year-old daughter cannot turn to her mother (parents) for help, where should she turn? She had made a mistake and had come to her parents for help and support. Undesirable as the situation may be, it still could prove to be the one thing that would weld an unbreakable bond of love between Christine and her mother, if Mable can accept it and rise to the occasion.

At the moment Mable is not concerned with Christine at all, only with herself and the embarrassment it might cause with her friends. Let's reenact this scene as it might have been done.

Mable: "Doctor, Christine and I have a problem. First, I want you to know how much we love this daughter of ours, and I am here to support her in every way. I'm sure you have some good counsel for *us* as to how *we* can best handle this situation. We think Christine is pregnant."

As it turned out, Christine was pregnant. A normal pregnancy ensued, attended by an understanding doctor; and Christine decided on her own, with no coercion by anyone, that she would place the baby for adoption. Later Christine finished school and married a worthy young man. But the most important thing she learned was that her parents were her best friends, especially in time of trouble. She will never forget the way her parents supported her when she really needed it. Would you?

Another case. Craig was just nineteen—blond and handsome, personable and well liked by everyone at school. No one could understand how he ever started with marijuana. Certainly he didn't need it. He was self-confident and seemed to have the whole world ahead of him.

Craig's father was prominent in the Church and community. It was such a shock to him to discover that his son was smoking pot that he immediately issued an ultimatum: "Either you get rid of the marijuana or you leave home."

Craig left home, went to California, "progressed" from one drug to another, and ultimately took his own life with a gun. I have purposely spared many of the details. But one thing I must include: The father has never forgiven himself for his impetuous gesture of kicking his son out of the house just when Craig needed him most.

Is there a better way? Let me ask you something. Have you ever tried to crack walnuts without shattering the nut? If you want a *more* nerve-shattering challenge, have you ever tried to crack pecans without messing up the meat inside? Impossible! That's what we had always thought until we discovered an old-fashioned, almost-too-simple-to-believe nutcracker that does just that.

Tagged somehow by someone as the "inertia" nutcracker, it is truly ingenious in its concept. To a frustrated nut-lover, it is a nugget of gold.

How does it work? I'm not sure, but let me give you the observations of an amateur. By placing the nut in a special end-to-end alignment, one pulls back a lever attached to a heavy rubber band. The lever is then released to come crashing against the nut that is buffered on the other end by a movable weight.

The resultant effect is *just the right amount of clout* to shatter the hard shell completely but leave the delicious nut intact, and it leaves a nut-loving nutcracker like myself exultant. All my life I have enjoyed the taste of pecans, but never have I found the solution to cracking them until now.

From this homespun contraption I not only learned how to crack nuts correctly but also learned another lesson as I watched it operate. Have you ever had to deal with a so-called "hard nut," a person whose personality was persnickety, whose veneer was like armor on a combat tank?

Have you ever had to deal with such a person on a delicate subject, one that might be explosive and shatter either your relationship or that of the group you represent? Have you ever encountered a situation in which your son or daughter stubbornly sustains his own silly side of an argument? He or she is absolutely, obviously wrong, but will not concede.

Stop and think! It is not a matter of right or wrong. It's a matter of ego, pride if you will. But isn't this situation similar to the pecan with its hard-to-crack brittle outer shell and its rewarding, delicious, tender meat inside? Yes, crack the outer shell (of rebellion) without destroying the nut (lovable nut, your child) inside.

Have you ever felt that if you could get through that outer shell of the individual without demolishing and destroying him in the process, you would discover a delightful, compassionate comrade —your child—inside?

By carefully studying the situation, by cautiously positioning the person (avoiding embarrassment to him) so that his feelings will not be hurt, then by applying the proper amount of pressure in the proper place at the proper time (with love as the guide), most outer shells can be shattered and souls opened up without damage.

Love laughs at locksmiths, so they say. In this case, love may be able to overcome hang-ups as it opens up hearts and saves souls.

Yes, we can learn a lot about getting along with our wayward children from the inertia nutcracker.

When waywardness has already happened, there *is* something we can do. We have an opportunity to learn, to grow, and to profit by the experience. What we often overlook is the fact that suffering and sorrow can weld an unbreakable bond between you and your child. Suffer and sorrow with them when this is necessary, but support them with your strength and your love regardless. Both of you may rise above the problem stronger than either of you were before it occurred.

PART THREE

THINGS ARE BETTER THAN YOU THINK

CHAPTER SEVEN

DO YOU EVER GIVE UP?

O ne day while fishing an interesting smaller stream lined with muddy banks, I reached down into the mud to retrieve and examine a rock that was lodged there. Dripping with oozing mud, this particular rock didn't look very promising. I dipped the rock into the swift current of water. As the countless colorful layers of rock came clean, they resembled "marble" hardtack candy. To me, once the mud had been washed away, such an unusual and fascinating rock seemed worth saving and polishing.

The thought occurred to me that many of our precious young people somehow become covered with the mud and filth of our society until they are scarcely recognizable as our own. Sometimes they follow their peers into such deep and overwhelming defilement that they seem unable to extricate themselves.

Then along comes someone who cares, someone who takes time to bend over, pick them up, and place them back into the gospel stream. Gradually as the filth is washed away, we marvel at the radiant, divine child of God who was hidden underneath that coating of gooey grime. How completely filth can camouflage something so lovely and so valuable!

When do we give up? Only when a person is no longer capable of changing. As long as there is life, there is hope for a change.

One day I talked to a friend of mine who is an orthodontist. An orthodontist, as you know, straightens crooked teeth. But orthodontics is a slow, deliberate process that requires a year or two of skillful professional help. Almost any tooth can be brought into line if we take time enough to correct it.

If the process of straightening is rushed, the tooth may be lost. But if we give nature sufficient time to adjust to the change as the crooked tooth is slowly moved back into place, the tooth can be saved and the correction completed.

Not too different from children who are out of line, is it?

On one occasion we visited a partially restored ghost town. Among other things that had been restored was the old blacksmith shop. In the shop stood a smithy with his bellows blowing and his white-hot coals waiting to serve him. In his tongs he held a straight piece of iron from which, he announced, he would fashion a horseshoe.

An engaging showman, the smithy carried on a running line of patter as he worked. One particularly interesting statement he repeated over and over throughout his demonstration. "You can't shape a horseshoe out of a piece of iron unless it is hot," the smithy said.

First he plunged the straight rod of iron into the white-hot coals as he continued to pump the bellows. Soon the iron was also white hot. Withdrawing it from the fire, the smithy placed it on the anvil and began to pound it rhythmically until it flattened to the proper thickness.

Back into the coals it went (along with his admonition about having it hot enough to shape it). Next he rounded the rod into the form of a horseshoe, molding it as though he could see in his mind the exact size of the horse's hoof.

Then it went back into the coals once more until white hot. Shaping the ends carefully, the smithy welded another piece of iron onto the curve to provide sufficient traction. After drilling holes for horseshoe nails he did the final touches of shaping—all accomplished while the metal was still hot.

Wouldn't it be helpful if we parents could learn that little if anything worthwhile can be taught when the atmosphere of communication between us and our children is cold? The warmer the feeling, the easier the teaching and molding and shaping. To lecture, to admonish, to discipline, when the atmosphere is tense and cold causes only embarrassment and shame.

The same could probably be said about anger. Anger often comes as a result of frustration because we think we have failed. But the truth is that we can neither claim the credit for our children's successes nor accept the blame for their failures. When we do this, we deny the principle of free agency given them by God in the council in heaven.

We can teach mostly by example. We can show the way. But when we attempt to force them, we are employing Satan's method. So you marvelous conscientious parents who have maintained an exemplary Christian home, you who provided the best training you know how, stop punishing yourselves for the fact that your children have gone astray.

Children who are so eager and anxious to take any praise and credit due them for good behavior must also be prepared to shoulder the blame and the inevitable punishment for their misbehavior.

I recall buying a chain saw so that I could remove some dead trees that threatened a Lincoln-log-type cabin we had built as a family in the canyon. Along with the chain saw came some explicit instructions not only for operating the saw but also on how to fell a tree in a desired direction.

After carefully studying these directions, I was ready to fell the tree in the opposite direction from the cabin (just as though I were an expert who had done it many times). It seemed so simple. You merely take a notch out of the tree on the side opposite the cabin and then make a deep, horizontal cut on the side toward the cabin but below the level of the notch. It was as easy as that.

For some reason it didn't work out as planned. When the tree came crashing down, it barely missed the cabin. But for a few perilous feet, that tree could have completely destroyed our treasured cabin.

I went back to the directions that came with the saw. Then I checked the notching of the tree. To my embarrassment, the notching was not at "true" right angles as it should have been. It was a little off center. The fact that the tree was crooked didn't help matters. The tree would also have had to fall uphill, which introduced another complicating factor. In short, the tree had fallen exactly where my notching, such as it was, had programmed it to fall.

Now, parents, our children pretty well notch their own lives. They determine which direction their lives will take. We have issued instructions, usually good ones. If they followed our directions exactly, their lives would undoubtedly take the direction that we had set for them. But their lives are their own. *They* notch the tree. We cannot do it for them. They determine whether they wish to follow our directions or make their own alterations.

They may have special reasons for *not* following our directions. But in accordance with free agency, they notch the tree. Usually they take the credit if their notching is successful. They should also take the blame if the notching results in disaster. But if they choose to ignore our directions and counsel, we must not become so embittered that we refuse to help them when they need it or ask for it. Perhaps it is our lot as parents to be "burned" and "spurned" by our children over and over, not just once.

Some time ago I bought a metal detector, and my wife and I have uncovered many treasures and had a lot of fun with this extremely accurate instrument. On the instrument is a meter that indicates how deep the treasure is. With it we can usually determine by the sound if the treasure is a coin, but not always.

Early in our experience we learned something valuable: Coins don't lie. If the meter says the treasure is two inches deep, for instance, that is how deep it will be if it is a coin. On the other hand, if the meter indicates that the treasure is two inches deep and we do not find it at two inches or slightly beyond, we can usually conclude that the treasure is junk. It is trash. Coins do not lie, but junk does.

In the Book of Mormon it says that the "Spirit speaketh the truth and lieth not." (Jacob 4:13.) If you inquire of the Lord as Nephi counseled his wayward brothers to do (see 1 Nephi 15:8), the Spirit will speak the truth to you and not lie.

Take time to meditate about your children. Don't just worry, meditate. You may want to go to the temple to meditate. You may want to fast when you meditate. But the Spirit will enlighten your mind and *tell* you what to do, even if it is only to love them. It will not lie, it will speak the truth.

I don't know how many of you have ever ridden a tandem bicycle, also called a bicycle built for two. Although ours was primarily for my wife and myself, I was surprised at how our children loved to ride the bicycle with one of us, at least while they were young.

Because the children were too small, we had to steer the bike. Wherever the parent decided to go, there the child went also. The child saw what the parent saw, heard what the parent heard. Whatever the parent experienced (or expressed), the child also experienced (and pretty well mimicked).

But as our children became older, they wanted to steer the bike themselves. And they soon preferred to take one of their peers with them on the bike rather than one of their parents.

Children, when young, love to be with us. They think we are the greatest. They imitate us, defend us, justify us. We are their models. They probably learn much more from us than we think they do. For this reason, we had better make good use of the short time our children are with us. We should treasure the time when our children are willing to go with us and learn from us.

Only too soon they are on their own. We hope they have learned enough from us that they will follow the guidelines we have given them.

In section 68 of the Doctrine and Covenants it states that parents have a responsibility to teach their children to understand "the doctrine of repentance, faith in Christ the Son of the living God, and of baptism and the gift of the Holy Ghost by the laying on of hands when eight years old." (Verse 25.)

Nowhere does it state that our responsibility is over when they reach the age of eight, but it does state that we have only the responsibility to "teach" them. It is the responsibility of the child to accept and follow that teaching.

So parents, get off your children's backs. And just as important, stop taking the blame if you have done your best. Stop punishing yourselves. The Lord mourns with you if your children turn their backs on that which is right. But he will be the first to commend you as he says: "Well done. You have fought a good fight. Satan may have won this round. But the fight is not over. Hang in there. Continue to love. Continue to have confidence that your children will eventually find their way back."

One mother stated that she kept up regular communication with her son through letters every week. Then she added: "And I always insert some little admonition or reminder that he should get back to Church and change his ways.'' I wonder how welcome her letters are when they constantly remind her son of his waywardness.

Remember the bird that tried daily for over two years to fly through the windows of our home? Even a birdbrain should have had sense enough to back off and take another look at the situation. He could have flown around the house to get to the other side.

See if there isn't a better way to accomplish the same end with your wayward child. Even God himself took another look at the age-less law of Moses and then sought a ''more excellent way'' through his Son the Savior. (See Ether 12:11.)

Back off for the present. Give up? Never!

CHAPTER EIGHT

THE FINAL SCORE

O ne night we attended a basketball game. It truly was one sided —against our team. Many people became disgusted and left early. I entertained the same thought as our team was repeatedly clobbered.

But in the last three minutes something happened to our team. I don't know if it was something the coach said or what. But our team suddenly came alive. Slowly, methodically, persistently, just as if a new team were being born, our team began to score. They developed an effective defense as well as an aggressive offense.

As the deficit between the two teams began to narrow, the opposing team called for a time-out. Back in the game again our team continued to whittle away at the difference in score. Slowly our opponents began to lose their momentum and their confidence. They missed easy lay-ups. They had senseless turnovers.

In a photo finish the game went into a tie and into overtime. In the overtime our "new" team outscored our opponents, and we won easily.

The real losers in this game were our own fans who became discouraged and went home before the final score was in, thus missing one of the most exciting games of the entire year.

Too often in our Church we view perfection as a goal to be achieved, and that is the end of everything. Yet what appears to be perfection to us now, may be flecked with flaws when we acquire the knowledge to envision a higher degree of perfection.

Perfection comes a little at a time. It is an ongoing process. We must not look down on someone who does not achieve that "perfection" at the rate we think they should. Nearly everyone is perfect in some area. Everyone fails in some areas. Let's not expect the impossible from our children or ourselves.

The Lord gives each of us a "key blank" and tells us to fashion it to open as many doors as possible. We are given some guidelines and told which doors will be the best for us to open. Some of us open wrong doors along the way. Some of us batter the key at times, trying to force it to open the lock when we have not shaped the key accurately. When bent and broken, it probably can't open any doors.

But most keys can be filed, shaped, and when sprinkled with a little "graphite" of understanding, made to function once again. The road to perfection is covered in places with loose gravel. Most travelers backslide a little here and there along the way.

In our front yard we had a large boulder that protruded from the ground and interfered with an otherwise handsome lawn. To my son was given the task of digging out this boulder and moving it.

After employing every tool we had, including a large crowbar, our son said: "Dad, it's impossible to move that boulder. I have tried everything."

"Son," I said, "you haven't tried everything. You haven't asked me to help."

Our Father in Heaven often must feel the same way when we give up and say that something is impossible. We have not tried everything unless we have asked him to help. And too often we place a time limit on the job.

The higher the building to be built, the longer it takes. Not only does it take longer to build a higher building, but the foundation must be proportionally deeper to give it stability. It could be that the Lord is just taking a little longer to allow us to dig a deeper foundation. Then he can help us to rise to greater heights as we encounter a few big boulders along the way that help us to develop our muscles.

In the Book of Mormon the Lord says: "I give unto men weakness that they may be humble . . . if they humble themselves before me, and have faith in me, then will I make weak things become strong unto them." (Ether 12:27.) When we consider the weaknesses of our wayward children, let's remember why the Lord has given them those weaknesses. They could become great blessings.

If you have ever washed windows, you know that you can see only the dirt on the outside (the other side of the window) not on your own side. Remember this as you look at your wayward child. Perhaps he sees only the dirt on *your* side of the window and has difficulty, at this immature stage of life, seeing the dirt on his own side. Just remember, you may have the same problem on your side of the glass as you look at him.

My wife brought home a music box one day. She is a connoisseur of music boxes, and they are one of the great joys of her life. This latest of her collection was unlike any of the others.

Every music box has a stem winder to make it go—so I thought. But this music box has none. I turned it over and over in my hands, looking for one—but found none.

With a smile on her face as she observed my bewilderment, she said: "This is a solar music box. It needs no stem to wind it. It is run by energy from light. If you look carefully you will see some solar cells in the transparent top of the music box. When light strikes those cells, the music box begins to play."

I took the music box outside into the sunlight, and it immediately began to give forth its most melodious tune. In our home we placed it where it would enjoy a brief encounter with the sun's rays at a certain time of day. And every day its music charms our lives.

Every child of God has within his soul the cells that respond to the Light of Christ. His soul has the makings of a marvelous music box. Our own love can help that child eventually permit the Light of Christ to focus upon the music box of his soul. The most heavenly music imaginable will come forth. Never give up.

On one occasion I was building a shed at my cabin in the hills. Anxious to finish before leaving for the city, I hurried my construction as much as I could. I had only a few more boards to nail when I discovered, to my disappointment, that I was out of nails.

It was twenty-six miles round trip to the lumber yard, and there was insufficient time left in the day to make such a trip. Searching around in the dirt, I found a few nails I had dropped in my haste.

But I still lacked enough to complete my task. While pondering my plight I sighted several bent nails also lying in the dirt. "I wonder..."

Taking each bent nail separately and studying it carefully, I discovered that I could carefully place it on its side, tap it gently in the proper place, and straighten it out. To my delight, I found there were many discarded bent nails that could be recovered, straightened out, and used to complete my shed.

Now, if I had tried to tap these bent nails on the head, they would not have straightened out and would have become even more bent out of shape, losing their usefulness. But a gentle pressure applied in the correct place helped them to straighten out. And the nails that had been bent and then straightened seemed to hold their place even better than the straight, new nails.

Often children are like nails. They become bent out of shape when someone hits them on the head too hard or in the wrong way. But the only way they can be salvaged is when someone puts his arm around them in the right place and with the right amount of pressure (love). Often these formerly-bent-out-of-shape youngsters become stronger than the straight arrows who came through it all unscathed.

I have often wondered what children really want from us more than anything else in life. The answer, I believe, may lie in the example of the Father and the Son. When the Savior was baptized and came up out of the water, the voice of his Father was heard to say: "This is my beloved Son, in whom I am well pleased." (Matthew 3:17.) Perhaps this is all our children want to hear us say about them. In other words, they really want to please us and they hope to hear us say that we are pleased with them.

We spoke earlier of life buoys—floating objects anchored in harbor waters. Such buoys come in many different types, but all serve the same purpose. They are to help ship captains and pilots steer a safe course, whether in harbors, rivers, or at sea.

Red buoys direct traffic to the left; white buoys show how close to shore the anchor may be dropped. Buoys with red and black horizontal stripes warn of danger spots, while black and white vertical stripes on a buoy mark the middle of a channel.

Lighted buoys clearly outline the safe channel at night. Specially colored lights on certain buoys warn of danger. The color and length of their flashes inform the pilot of special situations.

Some buoys are numbered and charted on a map so that ship captains at all times will know where they are. Black buoys carry odd numbers, and red buoys carry even numbers.

One thing is common to all life buoys: They are anchored in place. How totally unreliable a life buoy would be if it were floating all over the place! It would turn out to be a hazard rather than a help.

In a sense, we are life buoys for our children. Children look to us for direction. They look to us for stability in this unstable world of ours. Even if they don't take our advice, they still expect us to maintain our position. Without our uttering a word, our children know what we stand for. They know we will be in a certain place at a certain time. They pretty well know what position we will take on a given issue.

Whether we desire it to be that way or not, children look to us as life buoys to help steer them safely through life. They secretly admire our stability and reliability. They often look to us as their ideal person. They pattern their thinking after our thinking, their prejudices after our prejudices, their heroes after our heroes. Their attitudes are so often (embarrassingly at times) our own attitudes. Their standards are often our own standards. It can be a frightening responsibility.

But you can understand why it can be confusing and even bewildering to them if we change our standards and our attitudes. Children do expect to find constancy in us, regardless of any storm.

Small wonder that they often come home when they are in trouble. They know they can tether their troubled transport to something solid at home. But they can do this only if we are consistent, stable, dependable, and constant. A good way to maintain this constancy is to anchor ourselves to the unchanging principles of Christ and his unchanging Church.

When the final chapter is written in their lives and ours, even the so-called wayward ones, the final score may be considerably higher than we had hoped.